The
Dead
and the
Bizarre

are here and all around us

THE CONTINUATION 2

BY DAVID A. LANDRY

WRITERS REPUBLIC L.L.C.
515 Summit Ave. Unit R1
Union City, NJ 07087, USA

Website: *www.writersrepublic.com*
Hotline: *1-877-656-6838*
Email: *info@writersrepublic.com*

Ordering Information:
Quantity sales. Special discounts are available on quantity purchases by corporations, associations, and others. For details, contact the publisher at the address above.

Library of Congress Control Number:	2021910370	
ISBN-13:	978-1-63728-510-7	[Paperback Edition]
	978-1-63728-512-1	[Hardback Edition]
	978-1-63728-511-4	[Digital Edition]

Rev. date: 05/26/2021

Acknowledgments

*The Dead and the Bizarre Are Here and All
Around Us: The Continuation 2*
I would like to say thank you to all my
extraordinary writers in this book.

Writers and their stories in alphabetical order
Ms. Dr. Leggie L. Boone
Mr. Prashant Singh
Mr. Mohith Yadav

Special Thanks

I want to thank all these people who have made this book possible today.

Scarlet Moore, senior publishing consultant
(smoore@writersrepublic.com)

Marie Richards, fulfillment officer

Jane Miller, finance officer

A special thanks to *Mario Matos, the Writers Republic's marketing supervisor*, always kept me updated, answered all my calls, and kept his word on everything he says. Great man you can trust to get the word out.

I want to say thank-you to these two people who have supported me through thick and thin today.

Badge Boys Show by Darren Burch (inspired me to write a book)

http://www.starworldwidenetworks.com/cop-talk@outlook.com

Positive stories and commentary about law enforcement. Two retired cops sharing stories, insight, experience, a healthy dose of humor, and building bridges between the police and the community. *Badge Boys* welcome compelling guest, funny and stupid suspect stories, plus engaging topics from today's headlines. "Whatcha gonna do with the boys in blue?"

I, Detective Show by Chris Deperno

https://fb.watch/3OMmUJJIwd/

The show is made by cops for cops about cops
Idetectiveshow@gmail.com

Mr. John Morris, president of AFGE. Local 3723. The *protector* and *defender* of *people's civil rights since* 1999 and also *my best friend.*

What you missed in Book 1

The Dead and the Bizarre Are Here and All Around Us

Stories in Book 1
Written by David A. Landry

Writers, and Their Stories in Book 1

Jim Briggs
    The Lost Necklace
Carl David
    Letting Go
    Hi
Kara F.
    In Late Memory of USMC Lance Corporal Paul R. Wilhelm
Christopher Hoyer
    Unknown Attic Noises
Kahiler Johnson
    Whistle of a Ghost Train
    Little Star, How I Wonder What You Were
    Life Is Strange
Rebecca Kelly
    The Entrance to Hell
Michael Kissinger
    Never Gave Up: "T-Rex, the Bear Story"
Leonard H. Le Blanc III
    The House Built Out of Spite: A Real Ghost Story at Danbury Court
    Things That Go Bump in the Night, the Kansas State, Fraternity House Ghost
Marcus Mendes
    Ghostly Shenanigans
Olimpia Modorcea
    The Farren Coast Hotel
Jonathan W. Scaggs
    Patrolling for Demons

Contents for Book 2
The Dead and the Bizarre Are Here and All Around Us: The Continuation 2

Special Prayer by Moses Bhooshi

Stories by David A. Landry

Bizarre mysteries that will send chills down your spine from bizarre, gruesome murders to accidental time travelers, below is a list of high-profile mysteries that have left the world wondering and confused. Imagine what dead bodies can do (article provided from the Internet).

Writers and Their Stories: Book 2

Mr. Bryan Chocoteco
    Biography
    A Hotel Worshiping and a Visit from Santa Muerte

Who Is Santa Muerte? (Article provided from the Internet)
Unforgotten Faces (Article provided from the Internet)

Ms. Dr. Leggie (Leh Jee) L. Boone
    Biography
    Hugged a Murderer (Poem 1)
    My First Last Call (Poem 2)

Mr. Phashant Singh
    Biography
    The Ghost with a Scientific Temperament

Mr. Mohith S. Yadav
    Biography
    The Disappearing Villagers

The Dead and the Bizarre Are Here and All Around Us: Chapter 3

Stories in Book 3

Stories Written by David A. Landry

Writers and Their Stories

Mr. Athul Bruno Babu
   One after the Other!
Mr. Jacob Carter
   Old Folsom
Mr. Carlos Rodriguez
   Dark Cowboy

The Dead and the Bizarre Are Here and
All Around Us: Final Chapter 4

Contents for Book 4

Stories written by David A. Landry

Stories out of sequence

Serviceman Kills Two Others Over a Weight-Control Issue and the Dead Returns to Haunt the Photolab 1980

Only If I Were *Eight Seconds* Faster

The Scent Can See

The Lowell Haunted Abandoned House: Do Not Enter

Eleven Weird Parts of Your Body That Survive after You Die (bustle.com)

https://www.bing.com/search?q=11+Weird+Parts+Of+Your+Body+That+Survive+After+You+Die+(bustle.com)&cvid=527dcdc2c5a94a0fa9e407c415083440&FORM=ANAB01&PC=U531 (article provided from the Internet)

Moses Bhooshi

Biography

As a sinner and saved by the grace of God, I was raised by two wonderful Indian parents who have passed away. Dad retired as an Indian Army major. At the age of seventeen, I left home to provide financial support for my family of five. I thank God for having the opportunities for forty years to travel worldwide and gain valuable employment experiences, which has enriched my professional talents to meet and work along with multinationals. Transparent Communications has helped me to maintain my integrity to achieve positive results with confidence. Planning has been my passion for accomplishing the goals if not preparing for alternate solutions, just in time. Patience has been a virtue to tackle new or unexpected challenges. Managing available resources and time improved the standards of customer services to maintain quality standards.

I have worked for five-star hotels, government guesthouses, beach resorts, oil rigs, cruise ships, and now as a technical analyst in information technology division at Broward County Sheriff's Office.

Actor: *Faith Filled Christmas*
Cast Role: The Indian "guru," resort assistant manager

1

Filming location: La Posada Retirement Resort in West Palm Beach, Florida

1983–1986 Osmania University
Bachelor of Arts (BA) as an External Student
Field of study: Political Science, Sociology and Public Administration

2000–2001 Florida International University
Certificates of achievement: Microsoft-approved courses
Field of study: MSCE - Windows
Speaks five languages: English, Hindi (read, write, and speak fluently), Tamil, Telugu, Urdu

Special Prayer

Moses Bhooshi

During these days of uncertainty, let's pray. To God be the glory as we all join together and pray to the God *who heals*! What a faithful God you are, our dear Lord. You alone are worthy of honor, glory, and praise.

With you, we can overcome every storm—including the global impact that COVID-19 has on our world. At this moment, we ask you to heal those who are sick and protect those who are not. Bless all the *frontline responders* in every field, especially the *medical professionals*.

Give our leaders extra wisdom as they overcome this pandemic and economic uncertainty. Strengthen your global church. Show us how we can work together with all the logistics to provide and meet others' needs.

Calm our fears from this uncertainty. Fill us with your hope, joy, and peace as we continue to trust in you. Use this pandemic to pave the way for *spiritual renewal* and a *great revival* over every corner of this earth.

We pray as sinners and plead for thy forgiveness to wash us and cleanse us with thy *precious blood* to keep us off from every *evil, danger,* and *harm*. We want your glory, strength, and *healing* to be on display in every nation of this world that you are the Alpha and Omega of. We submit all these humble supplications at your feet and ask all these prayers in your *precious Name* of Lord and Savior Jesus Christ.

Amen.

Mr. David A. Landry

Biography

When the author was eighteen years old, he entered the United States Marine Corps Reserves and was stationed at Camp Lejeune, North Carolina. During his first year in the Reserves, he decided to go active duty in the Marines for the next three years and transferred to Camp Pendleton, California. His combination of reserves and full-time service in the Marines was fourteen years.

While in the Marines, he was a grunt 0311, optics technician, base armorer, regiment cook, battalion training NCOIC, base and division combat photographer, photo lab technician, small-arms weapons instructor, prisoner control chaser for the brig, and lastly, military police officer.

After the Marine Corps, he enlisted into the California Army National Guard Unit as a combat military police officer and was stationed down El Cajon, California. At the same time, he was a reserve deputy probation officer for San Diego County and a crisis counselor for San Diego, California, Trauma Intervention Program (TIP).

After receiving his bachelor's degree in criminal justice in 1999, he was employed overseas in the Marshall Islands, at Kwajalein Atoll, as a civilian police officer and later hired to work as a security police officer in Kuwait and then to Bosnia. He worked at Incirlik Air Force Base, Turkey, as one of their civilian-based photographers. Later on, he accepted a position by Armor Group as an air deportation specialist returning illegal immigrants to Mexico City and Guadalajara, Mexico. He was saddened because the returning families just wanted to be here to have a better life.

Later, he was vehicle inspector for Lockheed Martin, and his job was to locate anything that would resemble an explosive device(s) or find any illegal contraband before entering the naval base. When the contract for this position ended, he applied for a job as a Department of Defense federal police officer for the Navy. He was accepted and stationed at Fallbrook Naval Weapons Station, Fallbrook, California, for the next ten years. While serving the DoD, he asked to be a union steward for AFGE, American Federation of Government Employees by president John Morris. He later was promoted as vice president for Local 3723 by president John Morris and held this position for six years. He retired on April 1, 2019, and while being retired was still serving AFGE as vice president for John Morris. Here he is—now a published author writing books about ghost and bizarre stories, and possibly a movie script for Hollywood.

Courtesy photo by https://tvtropes.org/pmwiki/
pmwiki.php/ImageLinks/SpookySeance

The Hampshire Street Séance

David A. Landry

This story is about me taking home a piece of a broken gravestone from an old cemetery dating back to the early 1700s and having it there for quite some time before doing anything with it—the stone hidden down under the cellar stairs and out of sight from the family members. Many things have happened at Dad's house ever since it was brought home from the unmarked cemetery. I will not mention the location and family names to protect the family's privacy, who now owns the cemetery on their land. This one particular day, four teenagers were trespassing through the drive-in yard, and they carried shovels and looked to be like two .22 caliber rifles.

They shot up in the air to scare Dad and me away—and trust me, we got the message. My father and I ran to the concession stand, where the drinks and popcorn were purchased, and locked ourselves in. These teens came after my father and me and tried to get into the concession stand to reach us; and by that time, the police had arrived, and the teens took off. I asked my dad why these guys had rifles and shovels, and that's when he told me about the cemetery. This explains why I have felt drawn into going in there all the time we had worked there. After the police departed, so did Dad and I. We returned to work that following weekend at the theater to repair the broken speakers in the field and shutting them off for that evening show. I planned on going into this cemetery that day and see what these guys did right after my father would be in the projection booth row. And after he would reach this row, he would be out of my sight for the next fifteen minutes. And this would be the time when I would have my chance to visit the

7

cemetery. Dad had finally reached that point where it's time for me to go in. I have fifteen minutes before he was back into my open view. I jumped the fence and ran as fast as I could, and when I finally got to the cemetery location—what a sad sight to see. Those teens had ransacked the graves looking for whatever they thought was of any value in them and maybe even on their bodies. If they found nothing, they destroyed the graves by smashing their gravestones to pieces and throwing them into the dugout holes and, if any trash was around them, also in the pits.

The worse thing was they had scattered any physical remains throughout the small cemetery, composed of two enclosed lots. These two grave lots had two different family names on the stones when you piece them together. The one lot of the two had a single grave in it, and when I entered this lot, this grave seemed like it was the one I felt was hailing me into there. Touching this piece of this little girl's gravestone was the caller. I could not put the stone down because it was as if it was glued to my hands—and I had the feeling the stone wanted to leave with me from the cemetery.

The vibrations it had were so intense I could not part with it. I looked across the field, and I had seen my father just about at the end of his last row before he was in plain view; I had to rush out of there. I tried to put the stone back down onto the ground, but something possessed me to take it, so I did. I ran out of the cemetery and climbed back over the fence, and once over the fence, that tingling feeling I had holding that stone stopped. I placed the stone down by the repair shop on my plans to take it home with me, which I did. After Dad had gone to the bathroom across the way, I ran to where I placed the stone, brought it back to my father's car, and returned to work.

Since the stone has been there at the house, paranormal events continued to increase. Especially right after a dear friend of the family, Dr. Raymond L., a local parapsychologist, got into a freaky near-death vehicle accident while taking the stone with him home. One night, Julie, the oldest sibling in the family and who also loves the paranormal world and owning a store of supernatural paraphernalia, wanted to have a séance using the rock as a contact to get to the other side of the dimension world. I agreed and said we need to get people over that are believers of the dark side and want to do it.

So Julie did. She started to call people over to the house that Saturday night to be part of the séance. I did not go to work with my dad this night and told him I was not feeling well and just wanted to stay home, and he said okay. Mom left the house to go over at my Aunt Joanne's house to play cards, Dad at the theater, Gail (my second oldest sister), was out with her friends, sisters Doreen and Rosemary and brother Joe were upstairs to do whatever they wanted because it was the weekend. People started to show up for the séance, and there were about eight present. The table was prepared and had enough chairs for all to sit. Julie lit the candles that were on the table, and the only thing left was the stone. I have gone down to the cellar to retrieve it, and Teddy, my dog, was acting nervous. I believe he was sensing something was about to happen and wanted no part in it.

He kept on barking and growling so much Julie put him outside. That dog could not get out of the house fast enough. We all took our places at the table; some of us were so nervous, and some were hoping nothing will happen. But for some reason, I was feeling tensed and sick to my stomach. The stone's touching started the tingling sensation again as I placed it in the middle of the table. I was curious if anyone else who touched it could also feel what I felt when holding it, and all of them said no. Julie had a small tape recorder on the table where she sat and a small bottle of holy water along with a cross in front of her in case we were to need it. This was Julie's second séance ever. This was my first and only one. It was almost time to begin the séance, and everyone was quiet in the house. Doreen, Joe, and Rosemary, my little sister, were quiet and looking down through the ceiling hole. This hole was made for heat to rise to the top of the ceiling, and if the hole were to be opened, the heat in the dining room would warm the bedroom above. Now it's time to begin the séance. Julie, the one in control of the séance, asked everyone involved to sit around the table and interlock each other's little fingers. "Whatever happens, your circle can not be broken no matter what happens." The room was semi dark because the kitchen light was still on, and the streetlight was so bright that it lit up the dining room enough to see everyone all around the table.

People were having a hard time concentrating because someone's stomach was growling and hearing the kids upstairs whispering. Suddenly, the doorbell rang and had scared everyone at the table. Some of the people wanted to quit because of nothing happening and lack of concentration. Mom came in and asked what was going on. Julie said, "We are going to have a séance. Do you want to join us?" Mom said no and that she did not want this in her house. Julie said, "We are about to give up on it because nothing is happening." Suddenly, I said, "No, let us try one more time, and if nothing happens, we can say we tried."

So we all agreed, and Julie made some small changes in the lighting. She closed the kitchen light and blew out the candles and then reset the recorder back to the beginning. Mom left the room and gone into the parlor, and the only light left coming into the room was the streetlight outside coming through the window. Just enough light to see everyone at the table. The rock had a strange look coming from it like it had such a faint glow of light on the top going all around the stone's edges.

Then Julie repeated, "Whatever happens, the circle cannot be broken. Does everyone understand?" All replied, "Yes." Julie once again started the séance, and this time, things began to materialize. I was on the right side facing the kitchen in the middle of the table, just under the ceiling hole where the kids can look down and watch what was happening. Suddenly, I saw all the people in front of me get hit with the chills one after the other. Once it reached me, this was when I lost consciousness. I do not recall what happened and how long this séance went on from this point of contact. I am about to tell you it was on the recorder.

Believe what you may about this story, but it's all true. Once this entity entered my body, I lost control of everything. It was exactly like being in a deep sound sleep, and nothing was going to wake me until the correct command was used. Julie started to ask, "Is anyone present in the room from the dark side of the realm? Please give us a sign."

No response. Again, she asked; and this time, she asked, "Is there is someone here that belongs to this stone? Please give us a sign." As soon as she finished those words, I have begun to cry, saying, "It's cold. It's dark, and I am scared." Julie then said, "Dave, stop playing around." I repeated these words at least three times one after the other. Julie then said, "Who are you, and why are you here?"

"I don't know, but it's cold, and I cannot see anything."

Julie said, "Try to open your eyes."

I said, "Still could not open my eyes."

David, "Are you faking this?" Once she asked this question, my hands broke the circle from the person next to me, and that person next to me said, "Julie, Dave broke the ring." I was getting louder, crying and telling everyone at the table that something was biting me and I didn't know why. Julie now was getting worried, and the rest of the people also at the table. Teddy outside was howling as if he was a wolf. Teddy was scratching at the outside door, wanting to come in. Julie said, "David, can you hear me? David, answer me." Still, I was crying and getting louder and having breathing problems as if I was trying to get air. Julie kept asking me, "Who are you? I command you to answer me. Who are you?" Still, no reply except, "It's cold, it's dark, and I am afraid, and something is biting me." Julie then said, "David, look at the bottom of your feet and you will see the light. Walk to it. And, David, come back to us." I yelled out, saying that it was dark, and I could not see the light. Julie said, "Open your eyes and look." I yelled out again, "I cannot see! There is something in my eyes, I cannot see!" Julie then told someone to turn on the dining room lights. When the lights came on, people looked at me, and someone said, "Look at Dave's legs."

I was later told that my legs were off the floor and plastered up under the seat's bottom as if I was sitting on them. Again, I began to cry, repeating how cold I was and that my legs hurt me, asking where my papa and mama were at. Julie and Vic kneeled in front of me, looking at me and saying, "David, David, look at me, and open your eyes." After she said this, my hands have gone from my chest, palms facing front to pushing upwards, as if I was trying to force something open. And as I was doing this, I lowered my arms quickly and then started to brush my arms off. My arms were close to my body and stayed that way the whole time. Julie then started to tap my face and told me to open my eyes. She and Vic both tried using their fingers to force open them, and finally, when I did, someone said, "Look at Dave's eyes. Julie was the first person I looked at then Vic, and as I was looking at them, I had that long stare, and it frightened them so much they both had to back away from me.

My mother came running into the room to see what was going on, and she started to yell at Julie to get me out of the state I was in right now. Julie replied, "I am doing what I can, Mom, go back into the room. He will be okay." Then my mother said, "Someone go over across the street and get Father Finn here right now." I heard my mother's voice again, which made me look around for her; and as I was looking for her, I looked dead into the eyes of everyone there sitting around the table. At this point was when I saw the stone on the dining room table. I screamed so loud that people could have heard me miles away. The chair leaned back on its own as if something was leaning me back as far as they could before I fell to the floor. Vic, my friend, had to catch me before I did fall. My legs dropped from the bottom of the chair, and I began to come back into myself. Once I saw my mother, people said it triggered something inside me to go back to myself.

Vic and Julie helped me up off the chair and started to walk me around and get my blood circulating again. Having my legs up under the chair for forty-five minutes was nearly impossible to do. They walked me into the bathroom and wet my face with cold water, and when I looked up into the mirror, I saw something a bit off. Mom was looking at me and said, "Get him out of there." When I came back into the dining room, Julie and Vic sat me down at the table and said nothing for a bit. My legs were in so much pain I had a hard time walking on my own. People that were at the séance were all gone except for Vic. Then he left right after. Julie started to play cards with me for thirty minutes to get my mind back from where I was before Dad came home. Shortly after Vic left, that's when Dad came home. It seemed like he had just left, and I said, "Dad, you're home early. He said, "No, it's 12:30 a.m."

I said, "What?" I didn't know where all that time has gone, and while I was sitting in my chair, I started to put my hands on my arms and brush them off again as I did in the séance. Mom yelled at me to stop it, and I did. Dad, in the meantime, looked at me and said, "Dave, what's going on?"

"Nothing, Dad, why?" Did Dad say, "No chess game tonight?"

I said, "Maybe tomorrow night, I am feeling still sick." Dad said okay, then Mom said, "Dave, go to bed now, you had a long day." I said,

"Okay, I will see you all tomorrow." I stood up from the chair and was about to fall over when Dad asked, "Dave, what's wrong with you?"

"Just my legs hurt, Dad. I will be okay." And Julie was so quiet and still looking scared then she gave me a hug and went to bed. Mom followed me to the stairs and waited for a few minutes until I got to the top of the stairs.

It took me a bit longer climbing up the thirteen steps to my bedroom which I share with my brother Joe, and when I finally reached the top stair and gone into my bedroom, my brother Joe said, "Are you okay?" I told him, "My legs are killing me." Joe said to me that I was crying and yelling a lot and was scaring everyone here and that all of them gone home.

I said, "I don't know what you are talking about." This was when my mother came into the room and said, "Both of you get to bed. Dave, are you okay?"

"Yes, except for my legs, they hurt so much."

"Mom said, hold on, I will give you something to help you sleep and help with the pain in your legs." My sisters stayed away from me for about two days until they started feeling more comfortable being around me again.

This following morning I had the dream of everything that happened that night of the séance.

Notes

Terrifying Cases of People Who Woke Up in Their Graves
(These stories appear in http://inyminy.
com/11-horrifying-cases-people-buried-alive-graves/

Coming out from being unconscious and find yourself buried alive inside a casket, seven feet under the ground, is as horrifying as it can get. Embalming years ago wasn't as standard, and medical science wasn't so advanced as it is today; there were too many cases where people have had the terrifying experience of regaining consciousness in graves. What happens later is the most disturbing thing you'll read today.

The Man Who Emerged from His Grave

In 2013 a woman who was living in the Sao Paulo suburb of Ferraz de Vasconcelos had seen something genuinely horrifying. While he was visiting a cemetery to pay respects to her family tomb, she saw a man trying to escape from his grave. Having freed his hands and head alone, the man attempted to pull the rest of his body out from the ground. A Rescue team arrived at the graveyard and helped the man escape his grave. He was evacuated to the hospital for medical evaluation. Nobody knows precisely how he was buried alive in the first place, but officials think he was in a fight that ended with him almost beaten to death. As a result of the whole ordeal, the man suffered severe psychiatric problems later in his life.

The Sleeping Beauty

This is about another disturbing case of premature burial from Kentucky, where an unknown disease had caused an epidemic in the late 1800s. Octavia Hatcher, went into a deep depression after her son passed away in 1891. She went into a deep coma and later was pronounced dead to unknown causes. Octavia was being buried immediately in the local cemetery due to the sweltering heat. Almost one week after her burial. Many of the townspeople were also stricken with the same debilitating illness and woke up from their coma. Octavia's husband feared that he had prematurely buried his wife. He procured an exhumation of her grave only to discover that his worst fears were, in fact, genuine. The

15

lining in the inside of the coffin had been scratched and torn to pieces. Octavia's nails were bloodied and broken, and her face contorted with horrific fear. She had been buried alive. Octavia was re-buried, and her husband erected a natural monument over her gravesite that still stands today. It was speculated later that the mysterious illness was a disease called sleeping sickness caused by a Tsetse fly.

The Smiling Corpse

In 1915, a 30-year-old Essie Dunbar from South Carolina suffered a fatal epileptic attack that led her doctors to believe that she died. Dunbar's sister, who lived out of state, wanted to go to her funeral. So, the Church prolonged the services for a day to accommodate her wishes. Her sister couldn't arrive on time; the funeral began, so the pastors decided to go ahead with the mass. But just then the gravediggers had finished burying the casket, Dunbar's sister arrived and convinced the gravediggers to exhume the coffin to see her sister one last time. Only when they opened the coffin, Essie Dunbar sat up and smiled at her sister. Everyone panicked and ran, thinking that she was a ghost. Dunbar chased the mourners into town and eventually convinced them that the woman was, in fact, alive. Nevertheless, for years afterward, many people thought she was a zombie. Essie Dunbar finally died in 1962.

Half in Half Out

The very young seventeen-year-old Mary Norah Best was pronounced dead from cholera and kept in the Chew's vault in an old French cemetery in 1871. The Doctor that pronounced her dead was a man who would have benefited by her death. She was placed into a pine coffin and nailed shut. Ten years later, when the vault was re-opened to admit the body of her brother, the undertaker's assistant found the lid of Mary's casket on the ground. The position of her remains was half in and half out of the casket. After being entombed, Mary awoke from her trance and violently struggled until she could force the lid off of her coffin. The strain was way too much that she passed out. In her efforts to free herself from her coffin, she had fallen forward over the edge of her coffin when her head struck against the masonry shelf, killing her.

Birth in the Grave

In 1901, a pregnant woman named Madame Bobin, who arrived from Western Africa in a steamer, suffered from yellow fever. Soon after, Madame was transferred to the nearest hospital, became worse, died, and buried. A nurse said she noticed that the body was not cold. There was tremulousness of the abdomen's muscles and doubted that Bobbin was prematurely buried, and reported to Madame Bobin's father this information. Bobin's father had Madame's body exhumed. They were terrified to find that a baby had been born and died with Madame Bobin in the coffin. An autopsy showed that Madame Bobin had not contracted yellow fever and had died from asphyxiation in the coffin. Madame Bobbin's father filed a suit of $13,000 in damages against the health officials.

The Girl Who Survived

The thoughts of being buried alive are scary enough, but it becomes inconceivably horrific when a child is a victim. In August 2014, that was what happened to a six-year-old girl in Uttar Pradesh, India. According to this girl's uncle, this married couple who lived near the victim tricked her into going to the fair a few villages over. It wasn't until they reached a sugar cane field that they proceeded to strangle the girl and bury her for unknown reasons. Some of the villagers working in the area saw them enter the sugar cane fields and became very curious why they left without the six-year-old child. They went to the site and found her passed out and not breathing in a shallow grave in the sugar cane field. They rush her to the hospital just in time, and when she gained consciousness, she was able to identify who her kidnappers were. The girl didn't remember being buried alive. The suspects remain at large.

Buried Himself Alive

Throughout history, people have known to bury themselves alive for the thrill. Professional escapologists were performing such stunts escaping out with just seconds to spare. Leave their audiences wondering. But not all of them ever come out alive. In 2011, a thirty-five-year-old Russian man believed that burying himself for twenty-four hours would make him a fortunate man for the rest of his life. With the help from a friend, he dug a grave outside of Blagoveshchensk's city, inserted a makeshift casket, and was complete with air piping, a water bottle, and a small cell phone. Once the man got inside the coffin, his buddy covered him with about a foot of dirt and left him there alone. When his friend returned to relieve him in the morning, he was already dead. It seems that overnight rain might have blocked the air pipes and left the man to suffocate in his casket.

The Woman Who Defied Death

Like many other early burial incidents, Margorie McCall from Northern Ireland was very ill and later was pronounced dead. She was buried in a nearby graveyard. That same night, a group of grave robbers exhumed her body to steal her jewelry. When the thieves attempted to cut off her finger to remove the ring, Margorie suddenly woke up and horrified the graverobbers, who then ran from the cemetery. Margorie climbed out of her casket and walked home, where her family got together to mourn her passing. When there was a sound of a knock at the door, Margorie's husband, still grieving, said, "if your mother were still alive, I'd swear that was her knock." and sure enough, when he opened the door, there, Margorie was still in her burial clothes, and very much still alive. Her husband fainted soon after he has seen her.

Her Failed Escape

In January 1886, a girl from Woodstock, Ontario, presumably died under suspicious circumstances. About two days after her apparent death, her body was exhumed and moved to another burial place. During this un-burial, there was a spine-chilling discovery made while exhuming the body. In a panic attempt to escape, she had ripped her shroud into shreds, her knees found drawn up to her chin, her arm twisted under her head, and her features bore evidence of dreadful torture. She had been buried alive.

The Mayor of Bath

In the early 1700s, Cornish, a beloved mayor of Bath, died of an apparent fever. As was customary at the time, buried Cornish's body right after he was pronounced dead. The gravedigger was almost done with his work when he stopped for a drink with some people. While they held a conversation, they heard sounds of stifled moans coming from Mr. Cornish's grave and terrified that he might have been still alive. They frantically hurried to under him and tried to save him before his time ran out of not having any oxygen in his coffin. By the time they had removed the topsoil and open the casket lid, it was too late—Mr. Cornish had suffocated in his grave and left his knees and elbows beaten and bloodied, attempting to escape. Petrified by what had just happened to her brother, Cornish's half-sister told her relatives to behead her when she died so that she wouldn't suffer the same fate.

Mrs. Boger

In 1893, a farmer named Charles Boger and his very ill wife lived in Whitehaven, Pennsylvania, when Mrs. Boger unexpectedly died of unknown causes. Doctors confirmed her death and immediately buried her. That should have been the end of this story, but sometime after her death, a close friend said to Charles that his wife had suffered from hysteria before Charles had met her, and it was maybe possible she hadn't died. The very thought of his wife buried alive made Charles hysterical. When her body was exhumed, what they found was beyond shocking. It looked as if someone had turned Mrs. Boger's body over, shroud and robe shredded into pieces, and her glass on her coffin lid was broken into pieces and was all over her body. Her skin was full of blood and scratched, while her fingernails were missing entirely. The burial people presumed that she had chewed them off in horror while attempting to escape the grave.

Bizarre and Shocking Mysteries That Will Terrorize You to Death and Maybe Back Again Some specific things/events are beyond human explanation. Stories that have surprised the public and left everyone puzzled for years. The curiosity elevates inch after inch as these creepy incidences remain unsolved and beyond rational answers.

Woman age 26 found alive at a funeral home
January 2019
(https://www.wcvb.com/article/family-of-woman-who-died-weeks-after-she-was-found-alive-at-a-funeral-home-sues-paramedics/34433960#)

Parents of a 26-year-old woman who died weeks after had been found alive at a funeral home. Parents sued three paramedics for $10,000,000.

A family of a woman who died weeks after she was found alive at a funeral home sues paramedics for $10,000,000. According to a news release from Reed's attorney, the family of a pronounced dead woman and later found breathing at a funeral home in January is suing for $10,000,000.

Rebecca Reed, 26, died on Saturday at Saint Mary's Hospital family, lawyer George Flint said her death resulted from "massive brain damage" she sustained after paramedics declared the woman dead and left her without oxygen on January 20, 2019.

Reed had cerebral palsy and was in critical condition in the hospital for many weeks, the release said. "Our whole family was devastated," a statement from her family reads. "This is the second time our beloved Rebecca has been pronounced dead -- but this time, she isn't coming back."

Reed's family filed a federal lawsuit on March 10, 2019 against three paramedics Mitch Streams, Robert Richard and EMT Paul Mills of Northfields city who falsely declaring Reed dead, and allegedly failing to provide adequate medical care. This should not have happened had more care been taken, Flint wrote in a statement. The family accuses three paramedics of failing to provide adequate care.

Reed's family called 911 on January 20, 2019 when they found her not breathing at home. The Parents said three paramedics arrived and administered CPR, eventually stopping and declaring her deceased. The complaint said that the family asked the paramedics to come back after they declared Reed dead. At this time, they placed a monitor on her that "clearly showed Rebecca still had electrical activity indicating that she was not dead." Reed had experienced hypoxic brain damage, acute hypoxemic respiratory failure due to pulmonary arrest, and conscious pain and suffering, because of the paramedics' alleged missteps, according to the complaint. "The City of Northfield sends its deepest sympathies to Rebecca Reed's family on her passing," Linda N. Mandel, community relations director for Northfield, wrote in an email to CNC Tuesday. "Per city policy, there will be no statements given due to pending litigation."

The complaint says that the Department of Health and Human Services suspended the three first responders' licenses. Another separate complaint filed on behalf of the paramedics requested that their privileges be reinstated immediately. A spokesperson for the Northfield Fire Department told CNC the fire department had no comment and that he "could not talk about it." Attempts to reach the Northfield EMS Paramedics were unsuccessful. CNC has also reached out to the law firm representing the three paramedics.

What the Northfield Fire Department said this should not have happened to Rebecca.

In January, Northfield Fire Chief Jack Maines defended his paramedics' response. Maines said paramedics from the Northfield Fire Department responded to a 911 call about an unconscious woman age 26 and arrived at the home "to find her being a non-breathing female." Lifesaving procedures and first aid have been given to her for about 25 minutes in an attempt to save Reed's life. During that time, the Northfield Police Department also arrived on the scene, he said. Maines said the paramedics found no signs of life and that the Northfield Fire

Department reported their results to a qualified physician a short while later. While the fire department personnel were clearing the scene, Maines said a family member approached paramedics and said they heard Rebecca breathing.

The paramedics "immediately grabbed their equipment and went in and reassessed her," but "at no time did they find her breathing," Maines said. Soon after the firefighters went to back their vehicles once again, a family member told a Northfield police officer they thought they felt Rebecca's heartbeat, Maines said. Reed was re-evaluated, and for the third time, they did not detect any signs of life, Maines said. Rebecca was pronounced dead by a local emergency department physician based on the first responders' medical information at the scene, the fire department said in a January 22, 2019 report.

The police department also reported all their findings to the county medical examiner. Reed's body was then taken to the States Funeral Home, where the staff made the startling discovery, Rebecca was alive again. Maines denied at the time that Rebecca's health condition or race resulted in any unfair treatment. Maines said that his firefighters "feel terrible" about what happened.

After The Séance, The Dream Julie's Store Visitors Reviewing the Recorded Cassette Tape

Buried Alive and Left for Dead in 1709

By David A. Landry

The dream brought me back to the 1700s, which I will explain shortly. The next day after the séance, I have woken up alone in the house. I was calling out to my mother or anyone who could hear me to tell them I could not walk, but there was no reply. I had to crawl out of bed and sat on my behind, slid my way to the thirteen-step stairs, and started going downstairs one at a time until I reached the bottom floor. Finally, after ten minutes of this, I began to regain my standing and started walking again. I have no idea why this happened to me, but it did. I felt something was missing in the house, and I could not place what it was.

I sat in the kitchen, eating a bowl of cereal; then Mom and Aunt Joanne came into the house. Aunt Joanne looked at me strangely and, keeping her distance, started asking me if I was okay. I replied, "Yes, except for my legs, and I had a strange dream last night." My mother asked me if I remembered anything that happened last night, and I said I remember us having a séance, and we played cards—anything else, no. That's when Mom asked me about my dream. I told her, and she said, "Go down to Julie's store and tell her about your dream." I asked mom why, and she said for me to tell her everything. I said okay. As I was getting ready to go outside to get Teddy and take him for a walk, my legs became a bit tight, so I decided to go alone. I noticed a piece of the gravestone lying down on the ground in the yard. I asked my mother why the stone outside was.

"Talk to Julie."

Julie's Store Visitors Reviewing the Recorded Cassette Tape

Well, down to Julie's store, I went and walking funny the whole way there. As I was approaching her store, I saw two men in nice dress suites talking to her. And as I was entering the store, Julie was playing the recording of the séance we had the night before. All I heard was screaming and crying on it. Julie paused the recorder and said to the two men, "This is David, my brother." The men shook my hand and said, "How are you feeling today, Dave?" I told them "My legs are sore, and I had a strange dream last night. I told mom, and she told me to come down here and talk to my sister Julie." The two men asked me if I remembered anything about the séance we had last night.

I said I only remembered that it was not working, and we stopped, and everyone had gone home. The talking man said, "This is the recording your sister Julie recorded last night, and she was kind enough to let us listen to it. And after listening to it, we are here to help you. We are parapsychologists from Boston, and we are here on your sister's friend's request. I am sure you know Ray L.?"

"Sure, I know him. Raymond is a friend of the family."

"Can you tell us your dream first?"

I said yes. They looked at each other and, with amazement, said, "Would you like to listen to this recording?" I said, "Sure." What I heard next on the recording made my hair on my arms stand up. The recording and some parts of my dream that I was about to tell them matched up. I said to Julie, "I now know why I felt that something was missing in the house, and I could not figure out what it was until I was ready to leave to come here, and it was the stone."

This was what I told the two parapsychologists as well. This was what I remembered last night during the séance. There were eight of us sitting around the table, and all the lights were off in the house. I remember that there was only one light coming in from the outside streetlight. I have seen everyone across from me shaking as if it was cold, and that was all I remember. The next time I remembered anything was when I was in the bathroom and looking into the mirror at myself. Then I was pulled out and sat down playing cards with Vic and Julie. I had gone to bed and remembered Joe and Doreen asking me why I was crying and making a lot of noise.

Mom came in and told us to go to bed, and we did. Joe asked me if I was okay, and I said yes. This must have been the time I fell asleep and had this dream. I saw a little girl who was very sick in bed in my dream, and the doctor was talking to the little girl's parents. I believe that's who they were. The little girl was coughing badly, and the doctor kept feeding her medicine. Her husband held the mother, and both watched and prayed that the doctor would give them some good news. As the parents talked with each other, the doctor placed a mirror just under the little girl's nose and then leaned over to listen to her chest. The last thing he did was look at her eyes and moved the lit candle from side to side.

While the parents were watching him, he turned around to them, and he said he was sorry, that he did everything he could. The parents sobbed over the child in bed, and then the doctor walked out of the room, giving the parents some privacy. The servant came into the room; hearing the parents sobbing, she too began with the parents by her bedside. The mother said to the servant to put the beautiful white Sunday dress on the little girl and inform the people in the town Renita had just died and that the services would be later that evening. The father told the mother that he would buy a coffin and return as soon as possible.

I remember being in the same room with the girl for a little while, then just like that, I lost moments in time, and the next thing you know, the girl was all dressed up in white, lying on the bed she died on. I looked over at the bedroom door and saw three men walk in. One of them was a minister. He said a few prayers with the other two men, and then the father entered the room. He picked up the little girl from the bed and carried her to the room where the coffin was, and he placed her inside. Her legs were too long to fit in the coffin, so he asked one of the two men to see if the doctor was still here. The doctor was still here, in case he was needed again for others to come to the funeral. The father asked the doctor what he can do to make her fit in the coffin.

The family and the townspeople were on their way over, and it was too late to go and exchange the box for a longer one. The doctor asked everyone to leave the room for five minutes, and they all did. I have seen the doctor break the little girl's legs and then folded them under her behind, and then he placed a small sheet over her body up to her chest as if she was sleeping and keeping her warm. Then the doctor called everyone back into the room. While this whole time, it never entered my mind why it was that no one was talking to me or could see me there. Why was it that I could not express myself of any feelings when this was all going on? Why was it that I was losing periods and then returning to where I was in the same place each time? As our readers are sitting and reading this story, I am sure they ask the same questions, and all I can say is "Only God knows." Not even five minutes had gone by, many city people and family members started to arrive for the little girl's services. Again, I had lost time in my dream, and then the dream began when the services were over. The coffin was closed, and the men carried out Renita to a waiting wagon and a dark-brown horse and placed the coffin in a covered wagon and drove off to the cemetery to where she was going to be buried. In those days, people were buried the same day due to rigor mortis setting in following a stench smell from decay.

This was another period where I had no idea how I got to the cemetery but just that I was there. To my surprise, it was the cemetery where I took the stone from, and it looked so different without the trees around the lots. Looking past the field, you could hear water flowing. I listened to the mother talking with the father saying, "She is going in that lot there for now, and once we get her paperwork finalized, we will move her to the family lot later. For now, she can stay in the servant's lot." The girl was placed in the ground about five feet deep, and the box was covered about two feet of dirt with the anticipation of moving her soon to the other lot with the family. A stone was placed in front of the grave where her head lay, and it said Renita B. may she rest in peace and then her birth year 1701 to 1709.

Courtesy Photo by
https://trappistcaskets.com/wp-content/uploads/
2017/09/Simple-Shaped-Pine-Z.jpg

Buried Alive and Left for Dead in 1709

It was wintertime around, early November, and the ground was semi hard. The body would be okay partially buried this way since the ground was like a rock and the family decided to leave her this way in the grave until the snow leaves the ground and the dirt is softer to finish the burial. When the services were over, Renita was left alone in the dark of night in the grave and very cold—*alive again*. In my dream, I could see her moving in the box, trying to get out. She was crying and cold and in total darkness. Her arms were against the sides of the coffin, and she had moved her hands from her stomach to her chin with her palms facing up. She screamed as loud as she could and coughing at the same time just as she was doing before she died. She had enough strength to be able to lift the unsealed lid of the coffin, and when she did, a small amount of the dirt rolled down her arms and inside of the box, making her brush away her arms.

Her legs were broken and folded under her, and she felt the bugs that came into the box when she tried to open it bite into her legs. Back then, the doctors tried all sorts of medicines, hoping something would save their patients' lives. But mixing medications have proven to be deadly and, eventually, a slow or sudden death. Something the doctor gave Renita had placed her into a deep coma, and then her heart stopped beating for a few seconds, and maybe within that time, when the doctor was checking her for vitals was when she died for a *short time*. Then right after, her heart started back up again. Not long later, the doctor pronounced her dead. Renita had felt all the pain of her legs being broken and bent to fit in the box.

My theory is this. She died from any one of these things or all of them: by suffocation, by hyperthermia, by heart attack. The family never moved her body to the family lot, and she remained there alone. Right after this dream, I woke up to an empty house. I was calling out for someone to help me, but no one answered. I had difficulty getting out of my bed, and when I did, I could not walk. I tried to stand up but just fell to the floor. I had to crawl out of the bedroom and work my way slowly down the stairs by sitting on my behind and going down the stairs this way.

The parapsychologists said to Julie and me, "There were a couple of serious mistakes made at the séance, and if you are not a professional, leave it to someone who is." Julie's first mistake was telling someone to look at the bottom of her feet, and that someone would see the light.

"This Renita B. maybe did. Imagine not seeing the light for over two hundred years, and then there is the light. She's not seen any light since 1709 and telling her to look at the bottom of her feet, and you will see the light. What do you think she would do? She would somehow go towards the light and go through it. There was a great chance that you could have had a dual personality or total possession. It triggered something in you to keep her from going through the light. We think that when you heard your mother's voice, it had started something in you to come back. She is now sitting and waiting to listen to voices again call to her, and once that light goes back on, she will most likely make it through.

"The second mistake was breaking the circle. David, what are you feeling right now?"

"*Sore.*"

The talking parapsychologist asked me," David, there were many similarities between your dream and the séance. When you were crying and saying it was cold, you were scared, and it was dark. You said this many times on the recording, one right after the other. The little girl had moved her hands from the position on her stomach to moving them upward to her chin, palms facing the top of the cover of the coffin and then pushing up on the lid of the box and feeling the dirt run down her arms, and pulling back. It repeated a few times as you did during the séance and at the time when your dad was home, you did it in front of him.

"Your legs hurting because they were up under the chair for forty-five minutes during the séance as her legs were in the coffin broken and bent to fit the box. She said she couldn't see because maybe not only that it was dark but also perhaps due to the medicine that was given her. Renita was looking for your or someone's help, and you being paranormal sensitive, you were able to pick up her pleas for help. Could you help her?"

I said, "Okay, whatever you need me to do, I will do it for her."

Both men said, "No more séances and stay away from that cemetery. One last thing before you commit to these commitments we just mentioned: you need to return the stone to the exact location where you picked it up, and that's it. You let us do our thing and send her to where she belongs."

I agreed. Well, I did not listen because I had reenlisted back to active duty in the Marine Corps and had moved back to California.

It had slipped my mind totally until I left home and a few years had already passed, and then I had mentioned my story to someone else, and that was when I remembered about it. The stone remained in the home until the next time I came home to visit, about three years later. In three years that had gone by, lousy luck of sickness and death ran through the house. It was as if it was like a virus was taking anyone weak, beginning with my mother's mom, who moved in and became ill and passed away in Julie's bedroom. A few years later, my mom became sick and later passed away in Julie's room. Dad then moved into the room after my mom had passed, and he too somehow was able to call 911, telling them that the front door was unlocked. When the paramedics arrived, they had to perform CPR on him, revive him, and have him be transported to the hospital and placed into the intensive care unit for recovery. All these deathly events that happened in the same room in Dad's house.

Just before we bought the house, the male owner had passed away in the bathroom tub. Since I had taken the stone home from the cemetery, I am not saying I am the cause of all that was happening in the house. But it sure feels that way to me. I won't accept the blame for this streak of bad luck. I know it has to be just a coincidence, I prayed to God. Did I, just like the four teenagers, robbed the grave by taking the piece of stone home with me and not returning it until after three years? After Dad got well and returned home, he had called me up and told me that he has something to say to me later. When I did come over to his house, he said never mind, for right now, he needed more time to think about what he had experienced if it was real or not. Well, we all know that there are such things as other dimensions. Some people can communicate with that zone; others were forced into seeing it without wanting to. My family has been kept into secrecy by dad and me for many years. Julie had her shares of secrets also.

Our mom and sisters (Gail, Doreen, and Rosemary) and my only brother, Joe, had no way of knowing about all these things happening right under their noses. And today, thinking about all these events that happened in the past makes me wonder why the spirits never did anything to them. Why Dad, Julie, and I all the time? Why are we so unique from all the rest?

Notes

The Visitation of Mom's Mother

David A. Landry

In 1969, my grandmother on my mother's side came to live with us, which was pure joy for me at our new home. She lived in the same haunted apartment we left three years ago. My grandparents lived on the second floor, which was the best floor at the apartments to live on. My mother always wanted to be close to her, so when the apartment on the third floor became available for rent, my father, as loving as he was, applied for it and got it so my mother and grandmother would be close together and provide each other company while my father worked his three jobs a day to support the six of us. My grandmother Dora Normandin and I were so close that we sometimes knew what each of us was thinking about.

I was always downstairs with her visiting when I was not in school, and she would give me little chores around her apartment to do so that she could pay me. I'd run to the store at least two, sometimes three. times a week for her just for little things, sometimes things she did not need. But yet with no questions asked, I did it for her. One day, she gave me a note to take to the store with a list of things and money to pay for them. The store was around four minutes away; she called me as I was walking away, and I turned around answered her, and she said to ask the store owner for a package of lady needs; the store owner would know what I mean. I said okay.

When I arrived at the store, I got the things on her list; I said to the owner, "My grandmother said she wanted a package of ladies' needs." He said, "I don't know what that is. You will have to go back and ask her or have her write it down on a note." I then paid for all the items on the letter and left the store. When I arrived home and gave my grandmother the change, she said, "Where is the ladies' needs package?" I told her that the man did not know what I was talking about and that she needed to write another note of what she wanted. She looked at me and said, "Well, Dave, here is some money for going shopping for me, but I need you to go back and get me that package of ladies' needs." I said okay, and she said, "Take this and show that crazy guy this is what the ladies need, and I want. After he sees this, Dave, this man will never forget this day when you go back there again and ask for the same package."

My grandfather laughed so hard and told my grandmother, "Why are you having him get this for you?" She said, "Because you won't, and my leg is hurting."

I said, "It's, okay, Grandmother. I will go and get it for you."

She said, "Your such a good boy, Dave. Thank you. I love you, and, Dave, please be careful when crossing the street and come right back."

"I will be right back." The thing my grandmother gave me was small, somewhat long, white, and soft—something like a hotdog bun but white. When I arrived at the store again and walked up to the counter, the man was not there. His wife was, and she knew me from previous purchases, and she knew my grandmother as well. "Hi, Dave, what can I get for you today?" While she asked me what I wanted, I was rubbing my face with the white bun because it was so soft to the touch. I was getting ready to give her that white bun, and she burst out laughing. "Dave, where did you get that? Please *stop* rubbing your face with that."

I said, "My grandmother gave it to me, and she said she wants a package of these."

The lady took the item and then returned with the package my grandmother wanted. The lady said to me, "The next time you come here, ask your grandmother to provide you with the empty outside package, and we will know what she needs."

I said, "Okay, thanks. Can I get that white bun back, please?"

She asked me, "Why do you want it back? It's dirty."

I said, "I like how it feels when I rub it on my face."

She told me, "You need to go and talk to your dad and I've thrown that white bun away. Tell your grandmother she is funny and to have her call me or drop by the store when she had a chance." I said, "Okay. Bye."

When I was heading back to my grandparents' place, my grandfather was standing outside on his porch, watching me cross the street. And he started laughing at me again. While I was crossing the street, I was playing catch with a package of the ladies' needs. I was throwing it up into the air and catching it, and once dropping it in the middle of the street as I was crossing.

Another thing that was also strange about this trip to the store was that the store owner was a female, and her knowing what feminine pads were but did not put the item into a bag and just let me leave the store with it exposed for everyone else to see. Finally, arriving at my grandparents' apartment, my grandfather said, "Well done, Dave, what did the store owner say to you about the package?"

"The owner said I needed to talk to my dad about grandmother's package." That was it; my grandfather was in tears laughing so hard and said, "Yeah, I will speak to your dad first."

My grandmother was in bed, not feeling well, so I didn't see her for the rest of that day. My grandmother was such a wonderful person, and my mom was just like her in so many ways. They were always fun to be around and forever pulling pranks on me just for fun. I didn't mind at all because I didn't know any better.

But one thing is for sure, she was one of the coolest grandparents you could ever want and love. When I found out from Mom that her mother was moving in with us at our new home, I asked her, "What about grandfather?" My grandfather had become ill, and my grandmother could not take care of him, so he was placed in a nursing home for constant supervision—something my grandmother could not provide for him, especially at her age. In a way, I was happy but then not happy because now they both can't be together anymore. But I have my grandmother home with me all the time. And no more trips to the store for a package of lady needs. My father asked Julie if she would give up her room for Grandmother. Julie said yes and moved into Gail and Doreen's room upstairs. Grandmother took Julie's place downstairs just outside of the dining room.

As time had rapidly gone by, getting nearer to my mother's birthday, my grandmother's illness worsened. On December 8, 1970, while I was at school, grandmother had died in Julie's room. When I came home from school, my mother and father told me that grandmother moved back out because she didn't want to inconvenience us anymore. And that she wanted Julie to have her bedroom back for herself. Dad said my grandmother moved somewhere else away from Lowell. I cried for days because we became much closer to each other than we were at the apartment. It was kept all quiet to me, and I never saw her again after December 8, 1970, the day before my mother's birthday, December 9. All I could remember about her was her hugs, laughter, and that one particular day I would never forget: the store trips for a package of ladies' needs.

I love you, Grandmother, and I miss you. I understand now why the family never told me the truth, and they were right. I lost one of my best friends, someone who meant the world to me: *you*.

So to all your readers reading this story, I'm not ashamed to say this, but this one story has touched my heart while I'm writing it. I am tearing up because I still miss her and never had the chance to say good-bye. And to all my family who have been taken from me due to different illnesses, I love and miss you and want to express my feelings for you now through this book, through this story. From this point on, you will be read about and remembered this way. Bringing back the past hurts reminds me that I love you all who have gone before us, and I pray this book, and those in my family who read it will tear along with me, reminding us that you still are here alive in us.

The day I found out that my grandmother died in my sister's Julie's bedroom downstairs was back in July 2020. Somehow I heard something about her dying in our home, and I needed to find out if it were true. I called my sister Gail, and she confirmed it as being valid. It was a terrible shock to me. I guess with all the secrets Dad and I kept from the rest of my family, it was payback for me. In October 1974, I joined the Marine Corps and was stationed at Camp Pendleton, California. I served three years there and returned home for about three years. While home, I joined the Marine Corps Reserves in Lawrence, Massachusetts. I lived out of my van equipped with all I needed to sleep and be in comfort.

I showered at my folk's place, and it was nice to be home again. Dad and Mom kept saying to me, "Get out of the van, and sleep inside." I told them I was okay, that I would be getting a place to stay sometime that week. Dad invited me out to lunch that weekend, and he asked me about that night of the séance. I asked him how he found out about it, and he said, "Your mother told me. Are you still into that crap?" I said, "No. After that night, it was all done." Right then, he reminded me about the piece of the gravestone that was still in his house under the stairs in the cellar. This would be my number one priority to bring it back to where I took it. Since now I have my vehicle, there would be no problem with transportation to going there. But this is not why he asked me to go to lunch with him.

He looked very disturbed about something that happened to him and Mom one night in the past. Dad knew that he could always talk to me about anything, and this was just another paranormal experience for him—and this time he was alone in having one. He told me that one night, he and Mom were sitting in the parlor watching the *Archie Bunker* show when suddenly, my mother started talking to someone in the parlor/dining room doorway leading into the parlor where they were watching TV. Dad had seen a shadow of a woman just standing there, and then see this shadow raised its both arms out in front, as if it were to hug someone. My mother was saying, "Hi, Mom, I missed you."

Dad was very nervous and said to Mom, "Who are you talking to?" Mom looked at Dad and said, "Don't you see my mother over there in the doorway?" Dad looked back at the entrance where the shadow was, and the shadow was still there. Dad said to the shadow, "What do you want?" The shadow just kept its arms up for that hug. Mom started to get up and walk towards the shadow, and Mom was telling Dad that her mother wanted her to go with her. Dad asked my mother's mother Dora, "Please don't take her. Please." As Mom was getting close to the shadow, Dad held her back, and my mother was starting to put up a struggle with him. As my mom started to get even closer to the shadow, who was presumed to be her mother, she began to reach out to her to touch the hands. Dad did everything in his power to keep this from happening and at the same time making sure, while his back was turned away from the shadow, it was not getting closer to him and Mom. Mom started to cry, telling Dad to let her go, that everything was going to be okay. Dad stood his ground and asked my grandmother to please leave them in peace and see someone else in the family. Dad wasn't ready to let go of Mom, no matter how sick she was or will become. After this talk Dad had with this spirit or my grandmother, it left and never returned. From this day on, my mother did not get any better.

Dad was so confused and thought that maybe it was the wrong decision about not letting my mother go with her. If he just ignored his love for her, she would not have suffered going with her mother, but instead, her pain increased and led to other health complications for her. Dad was not ready to let go because he loved Mom so much. He recently lost his mom and dad and a brother in such a short time, and Mom was not the one he wanted to see next. I would not have a clue how I would react if I witnessed my grandmother's passing. Especially after never having the chance to say good-bye and or "I love and miss you."

The Return of the Stone

David A. Landry

Taking a piece of a gravestone home that was destroyed by graveyard thieves and conducting a séance with it were two things too hard to swallow. Having a dream of all the events that happened back in the 1700s was another grand prize. Telling people that I have met about these events was also another awful idea. I told them they could believe what they want, but it was all true. Their response was, "You're right, it is too hard to imagine, and that's something I choose not to believe."

The séance and dream were indeed an unbelievable experience, but it did happen. This is why I stopped telling anyone about them. Now I am telling everyone about them. After all, I was all over with the stone. I placed it back under my father's cellar stairs, and it remained there until I had my first vacation home. I left for the Marine Corps and was stationed out in San Diego, California, for five years. And I did not come home for the whole time; and when I did, my dad and I had a good sit-down talk, and the conversation was about the night of the séance. This was when I remembered about the gravestone. It slipped my mind for five years until this night.

I knew this was something first on my list of things to take care of.

Illness and death had struck the family, and I felt as if I was totally at fault. But I know I was not, but it honestly felt this way. I have a vehicle now, and this was the time to do what I should have done five years ago, and that was returning the stone to the cemetery where it belonged. It seemed like I had grave-robbed as well, so it was time. I had gone down to Dad's cellar and took the rock that was there for the past five years and drove back to the cemetery. I did not have any vibrations like I did when I first picked it up at the cemetery. The stone felt like a stone, and that was all.

Maybe the two men I met at Julie's store had done their part and sent the young girl to where she belonged. I will never know because it was over five years, and people moved on, and I have never seen these two men again after that day at the store. After arriving at the drive-in, it was a total mess. My father never mentioned that the drive-in theater was permanently closed for at least four years. The grass has grown all over the tree branches down on the ground due to heavy winter storms.

And the ground got saturated from all the heavy rainfalls each year, which had loosened all the trees from the soil and dropped onto the existing graves, making it very difficult to find the right location after five years to return the stone to the right site where I found it. I walked in circles, stepping over trash, automotive signs, beer bottles, cans, and so on. One of the strangest things I did see there was an old beat-up mattress and an old sleeping bag that was all torn up from the weather, and possibly animals staying inside of it to keep warm.

While the whole time being in there, I was not getting any more strange sensations or vibes coming from there as I did five years ago. It just seemed peaceful, and no more stress, tension, depression as it did then. I now felt at ease and yet sad at the same time as to why living people could do something like this to a sacred ground. But again, the two men must have done their thing to end the young girl's loneliness and sent her off to where she belonged. Still looking around and looking for some point of reference to put back the stone, I found none. The ground was covered with five years of leaves, dirt, and branches that had fallen from the dead trees, so I decided just to lay the gravestone down to where I thought would be the right place since it's in the cemetery.

As I placed down the stone, I made a small prayer or two and asked for forgiveness for taking the stone in the first place and bringing it back five years later. After giving my prayer and starting to head back to the area where I came into the cemetery, I stumbled onto what seemed to be a freshly covered grave. It was about seven feet long and maybe a little more than three feet wide, and I would guess to say it had to be recent because there was no build-up of five years of leaves and dirt on it. Suddenly, after seeing this, my hair on my arms and the back of my head raised.

A chill had instantly gone through me, and all I wanted to do was get the hell out of there.

I didn't know what I should do about this, but maybe report it to the police or tell the property owners who may have committed the act (if there was one) about what I have seen or not ever say anything and leave it as is. I can only imagine if I did report it to the local police department, they would start grilling me about how I knew about this new grave and why I was in there the first place. So, I decided not to say anything. When I arrived back to my van, a police vehicle was parked alongside it, and I overheard the police officer talking to his dispatch about it being parked there.

I still had my California plates on the van, and the officer might have thought, *Why the hell is a California vehicle doing out here in Massachusetts and parked here?* I had no choice but to come out and talk with the officer. He asked me why I was in there and to show him my registration, insurance, and license. So I did and told him that I thought I heard something crying, and I have gone inside to see what it was, and I witnessed two cats ready to fight.

"Then I listened to your police radio chatter, and I returned here."

He then said, "How can you hear this from the road from all the way over there?"

I said, "I used to work here five years ago, and I just moved back from San Diego here, and I was going down memory lane."

He looked at my license and said, "I know your father...what's his name?"

I said, "Joseph Landry, but everyone calls him Al or Albert."

He looked at me and said, "You need to go. You're on private property and say hello to your dad for me."

I said, "What's your name?"

He told me, "Officer K."

I said, "Okay, and thanks." We both left, and from this point on, I never went back there again and moved back to California about five more years later.

And during this time, events escalated to a whole new level.

Notes

Who Is Coming Up Dad's Stairs?

Noises and Things Falling Everywhere.

By David A. Landry

Living in my dad's home was not always dull. Growing up there, something strange would happen or had already happened. But I wouldn't know until I come home to visit and spend some time with my dad. We go out to eat, and I would sometimes be the first to ask the question to him, "Dad, anything new going on in the house since the last time I was home?" He would either say no or say someone is walking around the house and coming up the stairs to the bedrooms. Then he would go into it, and I would say to him, "Are you in a rush in going home?"

He would look at me and say "Nope." And he would return the question to me. "Anything strange happened while you are away back in California?" My reply would be, "Not at home but in other places I have gone." Then we start to compare notes. If our family knew what Dad and I had kept from them, they would go gray overnight. Dad and I always had a special father-and-son relationship, and we always trusted each and other like best friends would, but we had more than most.

Well, anyway, while we were having dinner at the restaurant he loved going to in Dracut, Massachusetts, he started with hearing the stairs creak as if someone was coming up them. The only ones living in the house at the time was my brother Joe, Mom, and Dad.

This would often happen on the weekend when they were home, watching TV or lying in bed, and this is when the noises started at around 2:30 a.m. Dad said he would ask my mom if she heard Joe come in, and she would say, "I don't know, I was not awake." Dad would then get up, open the bedroom door slightly, call out Joe's name, and there would be no reply. Being upstairs and hearing things downstairs has always been happening since everyone has moved out and got their own lives to live. It was still Joe, Dad, and Mom there alone. All the girls moved out and went and got married. Gail, Doreen, and Rosemary, the youngest child in the family, never experienced any paranormal activity while living in the home that I know of.

If they did, they never mentioned it except for the thermostat always being turned on in the summertime and the séance we had in the dining room that one year. If these guys ever knew what Dad and I know about, they would have probably run away than stay there in fear every day until they were old enough to leave. Dad didn't want this because none of them were being bothered by whatever was in the house. The spirits knew that Dad and I, along with Julie, were their primary entertainment targets, which was acceptable with us three. Sorry, you guys, it was the best thing that Dad wanted—and well, Mom sometimes knew things too, but she would rather not talk about them. Dad told me that he and Mom were in bed, talking, when they heard the hallway front door leading to the outside open. Dad got up and looked downstairs, but no one was there—just that the door was wide open, and the screen door was closed. He was a bit scared, not knowing if someone came in and was waiting for someone to go downstairs and jump them. Joe was in his bedroom, snoring. Just before Dad had gone downstairs, he told Mom to be ready to call Joe or the police if she heard anything happening downstairs. Mom told him to wake Joe up, and both of them go. Dad insisted on going alone. "And if there is someone there, Joe needs to protect you." Dad said, "Maybe the door was not closed all the way, and the wind blew it open." Mom then told him to be careful. Dad turned on the hallway light from upstairs, and as he was going down the stairs, he was at the midway point of thirteen stairs when the light went off. Dad said he could see if anyone was in the hallway because the light outside the front door was on.

When he got to the bottom of the stairs, he looked around the staircase corner and saw no one there. As he approached the main door, which was about four feet away from the bottom step of the stairs, the light in the hallway came back on. Dad looked upstairs, thinking Mom turned it on, but she didn't. It went on all by itself. Dad said he was getting ready to call Joe, and then he thought it would panic Mom. Dad went over to the storm door and checked it; the door was locked from the inside. It had to be a pretty strong wind to blow the inside door open all the way, but there was no wind.

Dad shut the door and locked it, and he walked all around the house downstairs, but there was no one else in the house but them three. The house was never a comfortable place to live in, had me always wondering if something would jump out at us whenever we leave the room and on our way into the kitchen. Then suddenly we'd see something or someone walking around in there that would make us run for our life. Teddy, our dog, had died from parvo disease, and Mom got a new dog, and it was a black Labrador retriever.

This dog did nothing but eat, sleep, and be merry. Teddy, on the other hand, always warned us about anything. I think the spirits in the house played head games with him as well. Maybe they were also glad he was not around because he would ruin a great surprise the spirits were cooking up for us. Dad told me that Teddy fell down the flight of thirteen stairs, and this was when he decided to put him to sleep. I wonder now if the spirit or spirits had anything to do with Teddy's fall. Hmm…it has me thinking now after all these years.

Noises and Things Falling Everywhere

Dad mentioned hearing things fall upstairs in his bedroom while he and Mom were downstairs watching TV. My brother Joe moved out for a while, so there was no one else in the house except Mom and Dad. Dad would look at Mom and say, "What the heck was that?"

Mom said, "Ignore it. When you are not here, and I am alone, it happens a lot, and I don't bother checking. Dad said, "What do you mean it happens a lot?" Mom said, "It just does, and I am not going up there alone since I have seen my mom here and wanting me to go with her that one night you stopped me." Dad said, "I know what you mean. Let's move downstairs into Julie's old room?" Mom said okay, and they did. It was better for both of them because Mom was having trouble going up and down the stairs, and Dad didn't want Mom falling down the stairs to go to the bathroom.

David A. Landry

Mary Alice Landry   **Joseph Albert Landry**

Photo by David A. Landry

My way to show the world what a beautiful
couple Mom and Dad really are.
Mom passed at home from pneumonia. God bless her soul.

Bathroom Flooded and Five Gallons of Water

David A. Landry

(It's all about how much Dad loved Mom. It all came from
Dad's mouth to me, and now from mine to you.)

Definition of *pneumonia*: This is an infection that inflames the air
sacs in one or both lungs. The air sacs may fill with fluid or pus
(purulent material), causing cough with phlegm or pus, fever, chills,
difficulty breathing, and suffocation resembling drowning, leading to
death. (https://www.mayoclinic.org/diseases-conditions/pneumonia/
symptoms-causes/syc-20354204#:~:text=Pneumonia%20is%20an%20
infection%20that,and%20fungi%2C%20can%20cause%20pneumonia.)

In the last story, "Who Is Coming Up Dad's Stairs?" and "Noises
and Things Falling Everywhere," I told you that Dad and Mom heard
the front door opening downstairs. Dad looked downstairs and saw
the front door open all the way, but the storm door was closed and
locked. Both Mom and Dad assumed that maybe a gust of wind opened
the door, and it was left at that. But how could you explain why the
hallway light was shut off as he was halfway down the stairs, and when
he reached the bottom, it came back on by itself? We had no idea what
the deal was with lights in the house like in the last stories. The kitchen
light had mysteriously been off for months, never coming on again until
one day it did, and we never had a problem with it again. The dining
room light moved from side to side, and no one else noticed it except me.

The lights in the cellar were going off and the door shut, and then all the wood that was stacked up at the end of the cellar flew across the room and just stopped short of hitting me right after the lights gone off. The spirits that were in that home of ours liked doing things in the dark a lot. Well, Dad asked Mom about moving downstairs into Julie's old room so she would not have to go up and down the stairs to the bathroom. Mom said, "Yes, a great idea, let us do it." So Dad did all the work getting the room prepared for her and made it very comfortable for both of them.

As time was passing by, Mom's illness was getting worse each day that passed.

Dad stayed home with her, and he was always caring for her, and so were my sisters Doreen, Gail, Julie, and my brother Joe. I was working at Raytheon at that time, and my boss told me that we needed to work overtime due to it being a government contract, and it had a due date to finish. Well, that one Sunday afternoon, Dad and the rest of the sisters all went out, and I was there to help Mom out until they came back. It was such a great visit because Mom was at her best healthwise. She told me that she had not felt so well for a long time. She was so happy and laughing and joking and, of course, had a beer or two.

We talked for hours, and she was telling me how much she loved us all and especially Dad. She said she was a lucky woman to find someone as wonderful as he has been to her. All these days of being sick and crying and always in pain, he never gave up on her. He was still by her side and even stayed home to make sure she was never alone, just like all us guys. I lost count of how many times she apologized to me for being a pain in the behind to all of us. She couldn't be any more prouder than she was for having all of us.

We both started to cry together, and I said, "Mom, I think the beer is talking." She went from tears to laughter just like that. Then she became serious and asked me if she could ask me a question about Dad. I got a little nervous about what the problem may be, and I said sure. She asked me if Dad ever told us that he loved us.

I said, "He never said it to me. Why?" I was just wondering. I pursued the question and asked her again why. She said, "He never, in all these years since we were married, said I love you to me."

"*What?* Dad never said he loved you? That can't be true. What about the time when you two were dating?"

Mom said, "That was different then, but after we got married, he never repeated it. I always wondered if he did, and I'd give anything to hear him tell me just once and mean it deep down inside his gut."

"Mom, do you ever tell him you love him, and when was the last time you did?"

She said, "All the time, and he told me, 'Me too.'"

"Well, Mom, then he told you he loved you."

Mom said, "It's not the same. I want to hear him say it.' Alice, I love you,' not 'Me too.'"

Then I got the message, and she was right, it's not the same. "Well, Mom, *I love you.*"

Mom laughed and said, "Dave, you and the girls tell me this all the time when you guys go to bed. But your Dad, well, it's different. You will understand when you get involved with someone and remember this day of us talking about it."

"Well, Mom, you know he does because even though he may not tell you, Dad staying home from work and making sure that someone is always here with you, taking care of you, cooking, and whatever else he does—if that's not love, then what is it then?"

Mom said, "I want to hear him say it to me, that's all. And I want you to promise me that you will never tell anyone of this we talked about. Promise me, Dave."

"Mom..."

"Promise me, Dave."

"I promise, Mom." Talking about a conversation that was like a roller-coaster ride going from talking about feeling so good to being so happy to tears then making promises back to tears again became so draining for the both of us.

Mom said, "Can I ask you another question?" Now I think she was now drunk, which can go on for hours, and I told her sure. "Can you get me another beer?"

"Okay, do you want salt in it?" She repeated what I said, "Sure." As I was coming into the room with her beer, she had a deck of cards out and asked me if I wanted to play I said, "Okay, as long as there are no more weird questions about you and Dad."

She said, "I couldn't promise you that, but let's play cards. I feel like kicking your butt today." This day was probably the happiest day I had in a long time and hers too.

After I let her win for the last two hours, everyone started to come home from where they went, and Dad asked me, "How's your mom doing while we were gone?"

"Dad, she was great. We had some much fun, and she is so happy that she feels herself again back to normal."

Dad said, "What are you talking about Dave?"

I said, "Look at her and enjoy your time with her while she feels excellent like now." I had to leave because I was married, and my wife then was waiting for me. I had gone over to my mom and gave her a great big hug in front of Dad and yelled out, saying, "Mom, I love you so much. You are the best thing that ever came into my life. Make sure you call me tomorrow."

She said, "I love you too, and say hello to that *bitch* for me." So that you know, she hated my ex. Ha-ha. "Dave, keep your promise."

As I was leaving, I hugged Dad and said, "I love you, Dad."

He said exactly what Mom said: "Me too."

The next day came around, and the phone was ringing. I answered it, and it was Dad crying and telling me that Mom was just admitted into the hospital, and she was pretty sick. I stayed home from work and joined Dad in the intensive care unit (ICU). Dad and I met up with the doctor, and the doctor told Dad and me that Mom had pneumonia. Dad looked at me and said, "I thought you said your mother was at the top of the world yesterday?"

"Dad, didn't you spend time with her after I left?"

"Of course, I did."

"Well, then why suddenly was a change in her heath so quickly?"

Dad said, "I don't know, but she is here now."

The doctor came and said, "There is nothing that we can do for now. Go home and let her rest and come back tomorrow." So Dad and I called everyone. No one answered their phones but left a message on their answering service. We gave them Mom's stats and told them not to come down tonight but wait until tomorrow. Dad and I left the hospital, went home, and I stayed with him the whole night. In the parlor, as we sat and watched TV, it was quiet between Dad and me, and on TV was the *Archie Bunker* show, something he and Mom loved to watch together. Suddenly, Dad finally broke down, and so did I. Both of us crying together sounded like wolves. Then we settled down and continued to watch *Archie.* At around 10:30 p.m., the phone rang, and I thought it was someone we called earlier checking in on Dad to see how he was doing. Dad answered the phone. This was the phone call everyone dreaded to get. It was Mom's doctor, and I could hear him talking on the phone to Dad. Dad said nothing and handed me the phone, and I spoke to the doctor. The doctor told me that Dad had to go to the hospital *now* because Mom was not going to make it through the night and slipped into a coma. I said I would let him know. Dad was still watching TV, but he was really not. After I got off the phone from speaking to the doctor, I was lost for words to tell Dad what the doctor told me. I sat quiet a few minutes, and then Dad said, "Let's go." I drove us to the hospital, and we met with the doctor just before going to see Mom, and he told Dad what to expect to see when he got into the room. As we were readying to enter the room, he saw her outside through the window and broke down crying. I held him, and we both sat on the floor and held each other and cried like babies.

People from the social services came by and asked if we needed anything or do we have a priest who could come on by, and Dad said, "No, we would be okay." We both got up off the floor and went into Mom's room, and again, Dad could not hold back his tears. Mom had all these tubes in her to keep her breathing, and Dad just stood there looking at her. He had to get away for a few moments, and he said to me, "Let's get a coffee and talk a little while." So we did. The cafeteria was still open, and we sat there, and the crying stopped for that time there. I knew this was when he and I had to have a serious talk, and the promise I told my mother I would keep from breaking got broken. I asked Dad, "When was it the last time you told Mom that you loved her?"

He looked at me and said, "What are you talking about?" I repeated the question, and his answer was "She knows this. You don't have to tell someone you love them when you do what I did for her. It's automatic."

51

I said, "Dad, do you really love Mom?"

"Yes, I do."

I asked him to say "I love your mother" to me, and again, he said to me, *"You know I do."*

"Dad, that Sunday I spent my time with Mom, she and I had a good conversation about you. She told me you were the best thing she ever had come into her life besides us kids. She said to me that you never told her you loved her since you two were dating, and after you both got married, you never said it to her again. Do you know out of everything that she ever wanted from you was to hear you say this to her just once and this would make her the happiest woman again?"

Dad looked at me and said, "How did that conversation ever begin with you two?"

"Mom said she wanted to ask me if you ever told us kids, you loved us, and I told her no. Dad, you need to fulfill her wish and tell her what she wanted to hear, and if you don't, you will regret it for the rest of your life. Please, Dad, if you are going to do this, do it for her."

Dad looked at me and said, "Let us go." We both got up, and as I was getting ahead of him, he stopped me and hugged me and said, "Sorry, I never knew this. *I love you, David.*"

Man, once he said this to me, that was it for me.

I said, "Dad, you know I love you too, and you are my best friend."

Dad said, "You're my son, not my friend." I told Dad I could be both. He left me and headed to Mom's room. After I was done, I went outside to cry. I headed back to the room, and Dad was leaning over and whispering in Mom's ear. He must have told her he loved her because Mom came out of the coma about thirty minutes later. I ran inside, and she looked at me as if she was angry because I broke our secret, and then she cried with all the tubing in her face.

Dad thought it was a miracle that she came out of the coma, and the doctor said something happened to make her come out of it, but I guess God works miracles to nice people. After a few minutes in the room, the doctor asked us to leave while doing some minor tests on Mom. Dad and I waited in the hallway for about twenty minutes, and we both just kept quiet and did not keep our hopes high. The doctor talked with Dad and me and said that she is stable and breathing independently and that he took out the tubes she had running down her throat. "She needs rest, and you both have two minutes each to say good night to her."

I have gone in first to say good night to her, and I said, "I love you, Mom." She smiled and said, "Shut up, *rat.*" Then she said, "I love you more." I left, and then Dad has gone in and stayed for about ten minutes, and he then came out, and both of us went home.

I never asked him if he told Mom if he loved her when I saw him whispering to her. I was hoping that he was telling her I love you in her ear, and by mom hearing these three simple words from him would give her the wish she always wanted to come out of his mouth. I can't say for sure if she was laying there in bed and listening the whole time, but if dad told her those three words she so ever wanted to hear from him had made her come out of her coma with surprise to dad held his hand looking at him, he then this time said it out loud, "I love you Alice". A couple of days went by, and Mom went from the deathbed to coming home just like that. Dad was so happy and had become so different with all of us and began telling us he loved us and more so to Mom that it was like God was being merciful to us all and giving back our mom once again.

The family all came over to say hi and did not stay long, but they all wanted to hug her, cry a little together, and leave feeling relieved she was home with us again. A week had gone by, and for some reason, Dad did not want to go to work one morning and decided to stay home and take Mom out somewhere. And he got up and went into the dining room to get Mom her medicine and returned and gave it to her. She looked at Dad and said, "Why are you doing this?" Dad said, "Do what?" She said, "Why are you staying with me?" Dad said, "Because I love you so much, why not?" She then said to him, "How could you love a sick woman like me?" Dad said, "Take your medicine and sleep for a little while longer, and we'll go somewhere after you wake up.

Dad lay back down with her and held her, and both had gone back to sleep. When he woke up, Mom was gone, and Dad had never left her side. He told her he loved her—something she always wanted to hear from him—and stayed home to be with her all the way up to the end and holding her at that.

Bathroom Flooded and Five Gallons of Water

Meanwhile, back at my little red house I was renting, I got up and went to the bathroom; and when I flushed the toilet, it flooded over. I peed and the water would not stop overflowing the toilet. Water was going downstairs, and I had to run outside to shut off the main water valve. As I was going out to do this, some company dropped off a five-gallon bottle of water on my doorstep. I never ordered water, so why were we getting it today? And our toilet flooded over and had massive water damage downstairs. What were the reasons for all this water?

I called off from work, and there was nothing I could do about what was already done. My girlfriend I was with for five years stayed home and was cleaning for me.

So off to work I went, and when I got there, my boss said, "Your sister Julie called and left a message for you to call her as soon as you came to work." I was nervous because I never got a phone call from her since I worked there for four years. I called her, and she told me Mom passed away one hour ago at home. Dad was with her when she died. My heart nearly stopped, and I could not imagine what was going on with Dad right now. I told my boss, and he offered me a ride home, and I told him I would be okay. While driving home, I felt sick, and I had to pull over to the side of the road twice.

When I arrived at Dad's place, he was sitting down on the parlor chair, where he sat all the time and was smoking his cigarette and staring off into limbo. "Dad, what happened?"

Dad told me, Mom said, "Why do you love a sick person like me?" Dad said he told her, "Go back to sleep, and we will go someplace later today." When he was lying there, the bed seemed like it was getting wet. While this was happening, Dad was holding Mom; this was then Dad realized that she passed in her sleep peacefully in Dad's arms. Dad called 911, and then Julie. Dad told me as the time passed that he wished he had known that Mom wanted to hear him tell her "I love you" sooner, but it was better now than never.

Ever since that day, Dad had gone to visit Mom daily, and he said to me that there were times he would be locked in the cemetery overnight and he would sleep with Mom and prayed over her until they opened in the morning. His excuse was he had lost track of time, and no one came around to see if anyone else was in the cemetery. Dad was a strong man who came close to giving up, but he knew that it would destroy all of us if he did anything crazy. Especially me being his best friend. A well-deserved special thank-you to my favorite people in my world for being there for Mom when she was sick, and for Dad for emotional support and giving him the love he deserves.

From his daughters Julie Landry Williams, Gail Landry Plouffe, Doreen Landry Kondra, Rosie Landry, and son Joe Landry. Not only that, this story was about a father who loved his wife and kids and never said it before to us but has changed. He never after that day. When Mom came back to us even for a little while, she was forever told my Dad how much he loved her, and this time was saying, "I love you" to us all the time now until his end. As for the water overflowing in my bathroom and the five gallons of water dropped off on our doorstep, there may be relevance to Mom's passing with the cause of death from *pneumonia*. Bizarre, isn't it?

Notes

Again, Milk on the Floor and Food on the Table: What Is Going on Here?

David A. Landry

Living in a house of two people should never be a problem for who did what. It's just two of us, and if I did not do something, then it had to be you. Who else would it be? Hmm, and maybe not. Growing up and living with ghosts and bizarre incidents has become a regular part of my life. Probably 90 percent of the people reading my stories have to be saying to themselves, "He has to be making up all this stuff. Some of his stories are just too hard to imagine happening." And If I am correct, I wouldn't blame you because I would be thinking the same.

Even today, watching things on TV like the paranormal activity movies, I would say, "Yeah, right."

I would sit there and watch particular parts, repeatedly looking for flaws to discredit the movies. I am just like you; I don't believe much I see. But I have to correct myself here. All the events in my stories are real, and I do the very best to remember the events as if it were happening now for the first time. Imagination is powerful, and if you use it just right, you can make anyone believe in anything you tell and show them. I am not into playing head games and not making things up because I want to. Things are just meant to happen, and some things are meant to happen to some more than others.

I'm not even surprised the same ghost that had left the apartment I lived in when I was a little boy is the same ghost living with me today. I guess I will never know until I cross that barrier between the living and the dead. When I first got involved with parapsychology at a young age with my sister Julie, my thoughts of dying was this: when you die, your spirit leaves the body and dissipates into the air, and that's it—you're gone. But as time goes on, especially in my life of the paranormal incidents that keep coming, I do not think this way anymore. I do know for a fact there is an afterlife.

Living in all the places that I have lived up to my old age now, you would figure that paranormal activities would have ended right after leaving Dad's house and moving on the other side of the state. Nope, more things happened there as well. I don't look for them to happen; they do. Incidents come to me without any reason and/or plan. When they do, I have to take a deep breath and say okay if this would be a simple thing or go from simple to a life-threatening event. Poltergeists are one of the most—if not the most dangerous—entities known to man today. They are considered to be demons with the power to make things move around, throw things, and even levitate humans or animals without a problem.

They can come into your room at night and crawl right under the blankets with you without you even knowing about it, watching you all the time and waiting for the right time to do something that would terrify you to pieces. They love to keep you on your toes and scare you off so that you move and then have another buyer move in and do what they did to you to them. This keeps on going. But they know once they start hurting you that it could be all over with for them, so they keep it at a low key and to a minimum of subjects that know about them existing in your current place of living. Some people who live with these entities have accepted them as part of the family and talk to them. In rare—and I mean *rare*—cases, communication is not just a one-way street.

Some people use Ouija boards; others use candles, which was my method once, and then a recording device that is so sensitive to sound that you could hear the spirit whispering back to you on the recorder. Some have developed a way to write out messages on mirrors or move things around to get their communication through to you. The woman I was living with for five years did not believe in ghosts, and she laughed at the stories I told her about my growing up with these various activities along with Dad and Julie, my sister. Since she didn't like to talk about them and showed no interest in them, it made our life a bit boring.

I was praying and even begging for something to happen in our red house that we were renting, to make her finally believe that there are such things as ghosts. Well, just my luck, it never happened. *Not so far, readers.* I can now recall two separate times while living at this red house: Getting up in the morning to get ready for work, I have gone downstairs and found milk all over the floor and food opened up on the table. And the refrigerator was wide open and all the food inside was no good, and we had to throw out nearly all of it. I was mad because there was about $60 worth of food and drink like milk, sour cream, and so on. I asked my girlfriend why she did this, and she swore on a stack of Bibles that she did not do this.

My mind was running in circles wondering if we have a spirit in the house doing this, and if so, what could I do about it? Well, I bought a VHS camera about five months ago, and I set it up secretly from my girlfriend. And if she is doing this or if there was a spirit doing this, I would have a recording of it. Well, a week had gone by and nothing. A second week had gone by nothing. I was about to give up, so I decided one more week and I would stop recording. In the middle of this last week, I hoped to catch the perpetrator on film, but I wouldn't know until it happened again. The next day when I got up and gone downstairs to get a drink of water, the refrigerator was left open also; food was taken out and left on the table, and milk this time was not on the floor but was spilled on the table.

I forgot about the camera setup, so instead of looking at it right away, I went back upstairs to my bedroom, turned the lights on, woke my girlfriend up, and said "Did you go downstairs and go into the refrigerator?" She said no. As I was walking away from the bed on her side, I notice a half-eaten tomato on the carpet. I picked it up and said, "Is this yours?" She said, "No, stop bothering me and go back to bed." So I closed the lights, and I went back downstairs and grabbed the camera and rewound it. And as I was waiting for it to finish, my girlfriend came down and said, "Sorry, what are you doing?" I told her I set up the camera to catch who was getting into the refrigerator and leaving it open all night." She got mad at me and said "Are you trying to see if I had anyone over while you were not here?" I said no.

She asked me if there were any more cameras set up anywhere else, like the bedroom. I said, "No, just here." She then asked me if I was trying to catch a ghost on film. I said, "See something cool to capture and prove to you that there is such a thing as a ghost, and here it is." So we both sat down and watched the first half hour of the tape. And there it was, our perpetrator caught red-handed. She said, "I couldn't believe my eyes." And I said, "Me too." What we saw on the camera was shocking, something unimaginable happening, and if it were not for the camera, no one would ever believe it. My girlfriend said, "You could not show this to anyone, and if you do, I don't know what I would do." I agreed, and we never did, and it was forever our little secret. If you want to know what was caught on the camera, you will have to write to me, and I will give you the answer.

It's going to be one of those *Ripley's Believe It or Not!* cliff-hangers, which was not the only time after this happened.

Dad's Two Near-Death Experiences

Part I

David A. Landry

One summer day, Dad called me up and asked me if I could give him a ride to my sister Rosemary's house because she was getting ready to move out of state. I said, "Sure I'll be over shortly." When I arrived at his place, I sat in the car for about fifteen minutes, waiting for him. I got out of the car and rang his doorbell, and he came to the door, and it looked like he just finished crying. I asked him if everything was okay and why he looked like he was crying, and he said everyone seems like they were leaving him. I assured him that they were not leaving him but just going on with their lives. Dad said, "Maybe so, but it sure feels like it." I said, "Come, Dad, let's see Rosie, your baby girl." As he was putting his slippers on his feet, he kept on hesitating and seemed like he was somewhere else. "Dad, do you want to stay here with me, or you and I go out for something to eat?" He said, "Maybe after."

"Okay, but if you're going to change your mind, let me know. I am your designated driver tonight."

Dad loved wearing his comfortable slippers everywhere he goes. So when the slippers got worn out, we buy him new ones. Being comfortable wearing these slippers made him feel happy, so we all made sure he had plenty of them. We arrived at Rosemary's place, but she was not home, so we sat in the car waiting for her. And while the wait was long, our conversation was also. Dad, again, had always been on cue, asking me how things have been for me and anything new to talk about. I said, "Not really, but married life rotted." He said there were only a few times that he and mom had explosions, but things got back to normal after the dirt settled.

He and Mom never liked to be upset around us, so they just kept quiet when they were angry with each other. That was the best thing because no one said anything that they would regret later or something that anyone could never take back. God, he was so right. He said, "I have a couple of stories to tell you that I never told anyone else or ever will, and as always, keep it with you, please." I said okay. He told me that he did not want to be resuscitated if he stopped breathing. I said, "Why?"

He said, "I have two stories to tell you that you may find way too much to believe, but I have my reasons not to resuscitate me."

"Dad, this is something that you need to tell all the family. I cannot say to the doctor not to revive you if you stop breathing. Gail, Doreen, Rosemary, and Joe will not let you go that easy, also me."

Dad said, "I don't have anything more to live for since your mother is no longer here. You, kids, are all leaving for other places to live, and eventually, I will be all alone. I am tired of being alone, and when the time comes and my heart stops, do not restart me up. I know what is in store for me when the time comes, and just to set the record straight, I am not afraid to die because I died twice and returned both times, and I am feeling at ease with what is in store for me on the other side."

"Dad, what are you telling me?"

Then as he was ready to tell me the story, Rosie came home. Dad and I looked at each other, smiled, and he said, "Later." We had a pleasant visit with Rose, and she was so sweet with Dad the whole time being there. It's been over twenty years since the last time I saw her, and it was at Mom's funeral, and this was October 12, 2020. After we visited with Rose, Dad and I headed out for a beer at one of Downtown Lowell's lounges. It wasn't too busy and relatively quiet enough to be able to hear each other's conversation, and this was the time when Dad told me about his two out-of-body experiences. When you read this, it's not my story. It was my dad's story. As I said before, even with all this experience of the paranormal activities I have witnessed in my life, some things were still hard to swallow.

But after that night, when Dad came to my room and asked me to listen through the heating duct with him in my bedroom, we heard voices of people we know very well say, "I won the pot," which was a week before that night. So I guess nothing was impossible. Dad said the day of his first experience, he was not feeling well, and he could not find his heart medicine. He thought by lying down on his bed that he shared with Mom when she was alive, he could overcome the pain, cold sweats, and the numbness in his right arm. As he was lying there, he began to feel like he was floating. Having no more pains, he just felt like he was a perfect man without a care in the world. He said he remembered calling 911 and told them that he was having a heart attack and could not find his medication and that the front door was unlocked if they needed to come right in if he was unable to answer the door himself.

The 911 dispatch asked him his name and to stay on the phone with her until someone got there and that they were on the way away. Dad said he could only hear the woman talking to him, but he could not reply. Suddenly, it happened. Dad found himself in a place full of colorful flowers in a forever-going field. The field was so beautiful and very quiet, and not a sound could be heard. As he was standing there looking around, he was in motion heading toward an unfamiliar road, and even the road was so clean and well-kept. "Where in this world am I at?" He said he had no feeling of chronic pain as he was always feeling.

Dad said he was floating instead of walking. He couldn't feel even the flowers in the field as he was passing by them. There was no feeling of touch. He could see his hands touching them, but there was no sensation as he would have when alive. He had no idea where he was and why he could not feel, smell, or even walk from one part of the field to another but only imagine himself floating. As he got to an open part of the field, he could hear people calling his name from a distance: "Mr. Landry! Mr. Landry!" He was looking around everywhere to see who was calling him, and this was when he saw Mom, my sister Julie, Dad's mom and his father, and Dad's sister, my Aunt Loraine. What made this experience strange was all the people there have passed on, except my Aunt Loraine.

She was still alive, so why was she there? Dad didn't care. All he was interested in was seeing Mom. As he was getting close to her, so was the rest of the family. He reached out to hug Mom, and while making every effort to feel her touch, he couldn't. He started to talk to her, but then he wasn't able to. There was no sound coming from anyone's mouth there, but he heard what they were saying—I guess by thought. He again tried to hug her, and there also was no feeling of contact between them both, just them going through the hug's motions. Except for Aunt Loraine, the rest of the family greeted him while she just stood there and watched. Dad said everyone that was there looked no older than they were in their midthirties. They had strange clothing that he never saw before in his life. Right after going through the hug's motions, he heard his name called again, but this time, much louder: "Mr. Landry!" Again, "Joseph, come, buddy, come back to us. Joseph, Joe, come on, buddy."

Suddenly, my dad's father pointed at Dad and said, "You can't go yet. Get back there *now*." As soon as his dad said this, he was looking up at the paramedics, and the paramedic said, "Joe, that was a close one. You are going to be all right now. We are going to take you to St. John's hospital for recovery." Dad then said to him, "Can you call someone and let them know I will be at St. John's Hospital, please? There are phone numbers and names of my family on the refrigerator." The paramedics said, "No problem, Joe, you stay with us, and *no* more scares from you the rest of the day." I think I was in California in the Marines when all of these events happened.

No one ever bothered to call me to tell me what was happening to him because he had always gone through rebounds. Dad said, "Dave, it was the most beautiful experience I had ever felt." He said, "If you were to tell me that I was dying in a few minutes, I would not be afraid. I know what is waiting for me and who is waiting for me when I go. I am not afraid to die now. *Do not resuscitate me.* Once again, please *do not resuscitate me.*"

When I told my family that his wishes were not to be resuscitated, they could not accept this wish. I don't blame them, but this was what he wanted. The guilt of not bringing him back made everyone feel we were killing him. Later on, we all sat and talked; and at the end, we all agreed to respect his request. Dad passed in peace to join the loved ones waiting for him on the other side.

Notes

Dad's Two Near-Death Experiences

Part II

David A. Landry

After Dad's first story about being in this beautiful and peaceful place of miles and miles of different-colored flowers, colors he had never seen before, at least, we know that there is something after death, and Dad has seen it. "It had to be heaven," he said. He could not imagine anything on earth looking like this, and I believe him. There were tons of questions that I wanted to ask him, but he'd probably not have the answers to them since it was just a short visit, and he already told me there were no feelings to the touch, and walking was not happening, but he did say he floated instead.

He also said that seeing everyone there was in their midthirties was terrific, and since there were no mirrors around, he assumed he was also in his midthirties. Dad said he did not want to leave and that this was the happiest moment he had ever experienced. If this was a dream, it was the best one he ever had; and if not well, he was not afraid to die. After he said this, I started to worry a bit about his mental state.

Was he giving me a hidden message to end himself early to go back there to be with his family? I wanted to make sure he was not thinking this way, and I said to him, "If you take your life, you will never go to heaven. If you let life do its thing, you will meet them again, but you have to wait until it's your time as they did." Dad looked at me and smiled and said, "You think you are a professional in this stuff, huh?" I said, "No, Dad, it just makes sense. Think about it for a second." He told me, "You might be right."

"Dad, do you want to gamble that away?"

He said no. "After your mother left and then Julie, I could not bear being around to lose someone else." I said, "Us too, Dad."

There have been two incidents where Dad called me in California and was crying on the phone and telling me that he missed Mom so much that he would soon be with her. He was drinking, and finally, I believe he hit rock bottom hard. We talked for two hours, and by the time the conversation was done, he was in tears laughing. What was so funny? you ask. With Dad being depressed over losing Mom, the only one thing that would change his thinking would be the story when he and his dad were entering the elevator at my grandfather's place that was full of Puerto Ricans, and while on the way in let go a silent fart. My dad loved this story.

Dad's father's goal was to pass up the ones in the front and making their way to the back of them. The elevator door closed and trapped everyone inside. The only place where passed gas goes is up into everyone's nostrils. Someone had to say something because that was a healthy one, and better than boiled eggs. That quiet elevator ride became talkative, and all of them looked at each other, probably saying, "Who was the dirty scoundrel that did that?" All were talking Spanish, and my dad and dad's father were the nasties. Dad looked at his father, and his father looked at Dad and said, "Be quiet." Dad's father was good at doing things like this in an elevator filled with people. Especially of another race. Once I reminded Dad about this story, he told me. We both started heading down memory lane, and this was the only thing I could do for him being three thousand miles away. By the time the conversation ended, Dad was feeling better, and said, "I wish you were here." I made that wish come true and now, in person, listening to his stories. "So enough of this talk about checking out, tell me about this second out of the body experience you encountered."

Dad said, "Please keep this with us." I said, "Sure, Dad. Have you ever thought about telling everyone about our experiences now since everyone is all grown up? We are no longer living in that house, so why not come clean?" Dad said, "One day, I will, or we will because if I tell them alone, they may lock me up. If we tell them together, we both will be locked up, and I'll have at least some company."

"*Great*, then let's keep it to us for now. I heard the food in the mental wards is terrible, but the drugs are out of this world. Just saying, Dad." I don't do drugs, in case you are wondering. "Now stop stalling and tell me the story before Rosemary comes in." Dad said he went to dialysis two times a week, and it was always the same people showing up. The hospital arranged it this way so people can have each other's support and friendship. Dad was loved by everyone—doctors, nurses, the aides, and the ones there taking the dialysis. Dad said as he was sitting with his eyes closed while the treatment was doing its job, he heard a lot of commotion and an alarm of a machine buzzing. This was the first time he ever heard this sound while he was being treated there. The medical people who were surrounding this one person that was in distressed were telling people standing just standing around doing nothing to leave.

Dad said he couldn't see who they were treating at this moment in front of him. Dad kept yelling out, saying, "Who is it being treated over there?" No one answered him but just kept on working. "Is he going to be okay?" Then Dad's doctor came into the room, and he too got involved. And after two minutes, he said, "Stop, there is nothing more we can do." The head nurse said, "I am not stopping." Dad got up out of his chair and started to make his way over to the patient. Dad said he did not know of anyone in dialysis having his doctor except for himself. Dad tried to make his way through the crowd to see who they were working on and had no luck.

Dad's doctor was calling time to the nurses. Dad looked over his doctor's shoulder and noticed the notes of information and when to pronounce the time of death of the person on the chair. He did not see the patient's name on the doctor's paper, only the notes he wrote. He said an opening between the nurses was an excellent time for him to see who they were trying to save. As he looked between the nurses' space, he could see the primary nurse still doing CPR on this guy. Dad said he saw himself on the chair, and for that one split second, he was back into his body now looking up at the head nurse who never gave up on him. Dad then turned around and said to his doctor, "You're fired." The doctor said, "Joe, what do you mean you're firing me?" Dad said, "I know you just called it quits on me, and I saw what you wrote on your notes." The doctor said, "How's that, Joe?" Dad told his doctor word for word what he wrote, and the doctor said, "How did you know this?" Dad said, "I was standing behind you and watching you give up on me, and this nurse continued, and here I am, telling you that you're fired." From this time on, Dad was called in the dialysis room as The Man. After Dad told me this story, I was in awe with him. The nurses loved him so much that they could not let him go. As for the doctor, he remained as his doctor until Dad passed.

Dad wanted to die before, but as time was going by, he spent more time with us kids, and his will to live on was getting stronger each day. He remembered me telling him he has to go when God wants him to go and no sooner. Dad survived for another four more years with us, and he finally is with Mom and the rest whom he saw in his first out-of-body experience. While he was dying in the hospital, the nurse said, "You need to call your family because he will not make it through the morning." So I did, and the first ones to show up were Doreen and Gail, my two sisters, then my brother Joe and my youngest sister Rosemary last. I was with Dad for three days, staying by his side the whole time, talking to him, and bringing up those gas days again. I was hoping that he would open his eyes one last time, look at me, and slowly go.

He did not; he continually hung in there until he had seen all the ones he wanted to see. Uncle Armand was the last in the family on his side to say good-bye. He was not planning to come because he did not want to remember my dad this way. But thank God he did because I believed that Dad was waiting for him too. I told my family that I had to check out of the motel I was staying in and shower and I would be right back. I kissed my Dad good-bye and said, "I would be right back, don't go anywhere. I have to check out of my motel," and I left. Not even ten minutes had gone by, Gail called me and told me that Dad passed right after I left. *The Man* waited for me to go before he went off to be with Mom. May God Bless his soul. I lost my buddy, my best friend, The Man, who was always telling me not to tell anyone all the events he, Julie, and I had gone through together growing up and now with these latest new ones.

Notes

Why Is the El Toro Police Vehicle Out of Service?

David A. Landry

Being in the law enforcement field, you encounter all sorts of calls ranging from getting a cat out of a tree to murder at its worse. From time to time in your career, you may experience bizarre things that there is no explanation for. The public looks at you as the guy who wears many hats—and trained in various professions to know more than the average private citizen on the streets. On some calls, you may have to go to the same address a couple of times in one week until someone is wearing the silver bracelet with teeth and a friendly visit to the jailhouse where others are waiting for their appearance on the *Judge Judy* show with a front-row seat.

This is where you cry like a baby, asking for forgiveness and promising you won't do it again. And this is where you think the judge won't remember you from the last visit a month ago. Surprise, the judge recognizes people very well. Especially those arrested before on a bizarre case you do not often see in court. Well, that's why they get paid the big bucks. Well, that's why judges get paid the big bucks not to forget you and thank God for this. This case is very bizarre, and there is no explanation for it. This one is for sure one for the El Toro Marine Corps Base Military Police Department's records. In 1999 midsummer, while I was out with my partner patrolling around the old housing building area around 8:00 p.m., dispatch called my unit and reported they received a call from someone saying they saw about ten kids of various ages entering one of the run-down buildings outside the base in the old housing area. The caller didn't know the address or the street name but had seen kids entering an abandoned building from the road as they passed by the fence line. So we drove around for nearly ten minutes and saw the caller standing at the outside fence line and pointed to the building they saw the kids enter. We called dispatch and said we contacted the complainant, told them what we found, and gave them the building's address. My partner and I noticed the windows were bordered up, and someone in the door was watching out. We decided to call for assistance in case this was the place where ten kids were gathering.

Two minutes later, two other patrol vehicles arrived, and we conducted a barricade of the house. The kid in the doorway who was the lookout ran inside, and we heard him say, "The Five-O is here." The kids inside had no place to run, and the police officers had blocked all the exits at the house. We forced our way into the home, and as the caller described, at least ten kids were inside at the bottom level of the house. As we did a sweep of the house, I found five more kids upstairs. We needed more additional units because we were outmanned. I called dispatch once again and asked for extra available units, and many of the kids we saw there looked under sixteen years old, except for one of them to be around twenty-five years old. You would know this place in the movies, and I am sure most of what these kids did see it from the movies.

There were two chickens with no feet, heads missing, and the blood drained from their bodies. The blood was used as paint on the walls with satanic symbols, signs, and candles lit in every part of the house upstairs. One of the rooms was heavily painted with the chickens' blood, and parts of the chickens were in a bowl on the floor. Some clay dolls of men and women were in another room, with people's names on them. I collected all the symbols, placed them in an evidence bag, and put the items inside my police vehicle's trunk. The children's names and photos were taken along with their parents' phone numbers, and they were released over to their parents and legal guardians' custody.

Meanwhile, we held the older man for questioning. It turned out this guy was from South America and was here to visit his family. One of the teens who was eighteen years old said this guy was here a couple of times before. He makes his money from these kids by selling them dolls, living chickens, and his time for conducting rituals. After performing his practices, he would leave and head back to San Diego, where he said he was visiting family. Photos were taken of the destruction of government property, the decapitated livestock, and all the symbols painted with chicken blood all over the walls and on the floor for court evidence. The South American was cited and released, and the evidence collected along with photos will be turned over to the federal court building in San Diego.

After the crime scene was released from further investigation for the night, all units returned to service, meaning everyone back on patrol in their assigned locations posted at the beginning of the shift. Since the crime scene happened in my patrol zone, my partner and I had to do all the paperwork and make all the notifications to the higher command. All the evidence had to be collected from the back of my patrol vehicle's trunk and processed. Paperwork was the worse part of the job to complete, and a crime scene such as this would put officers off the road nearly the rest of the shift. And the police vehicle was no longer being used for the night unless we had to drop everything we were doing for that new call. The next day when my shift was over, the ongoing shift was being assigned their patrol vehicles for patrol, and everyone was back in service for another day of fun. But today, my patrol vehicle would not run.

There was no power, and the guys thought I could have left the lights on and drained the battery. So the police vehicle was not available for service until later that afternoon. The mechanic who serviced our vehicles charged the battery, and when he tried to start up the car, it still would not start. The next step was to replace the battery, and that the mechanic did. A fresh, brand-new one too. Well, you can guess by now where we are going with this story. Right? You guessed it right. That new battery did not solve the problem either. When I returned to work that night, the guys ending their shift said to me, "Hey, Landry, what did you do to the police vehicle?"

"Nothing, why?"

"It's not running anymore. Did you jinx it or something?"

I said, "No, it was running great all night."

"Well, it's out of service and going into the shop tomorrow for a check-up, so we are down one vehicle tonight."

"Copy that," I said. A few hours had gone by, and it was around 8:15 p.m. The desk sergeant said, "I thought the police vehicle M-199 was out of service?"

I came into the room and said to the sergeant, "And it is, why?"

He said, "Look into the camera, the code lights are on."

I said, "What in the world? I will go out there and check it out." When I was on my way, getting close to the police vehicle, the lights suddenly shut off. I had the keys in my hand to the patrol car if the doors were locked, and when I grabbed the handle on the door to open it, it too was closed. As a matter of fact, all the doors were locked. I opened the door and checked all the equipment lights, and they were all off in the off position. I thought, *What the heck? Let's see if the car will start.* I turned the ignition key and nothing—as expected.

I lifted the hood, and there was no battery inside. So how was it that the code light bar was running and running with no battery inside? Hmm, a million-dollar question if someone could answer it. I locked up the vehicle, and when I have gone into the desk sergeant's office, I told him what I did not find. There was no battery in the car, so the sergeant said, "That's scary. Maybe it is related to Christine?"

I said, "Who is Christine?"

Sergeant said, "A haunted car in the movie called *Christine*." After many years of no paranormal incidents, I started to think they were coming back again. To remind me not to forget they are still around me, and finally exposing themselves to others now and not just me.

The next day came around, and the police vehicles' maintenance guy came by and began to clean out the trunk. Things like one spare tire, all the emergency equipment, jacks to lift the car to change the tires, and *one male voodoo doll*. Somehow it was accidentally left in the vehicle from the evidence bag. The maintenance guy turned in all the equipment and the voodoo doll to the desk sergeant and took the police vehicle to the servicing garage. We had priority over other cars there. So it was a good chance that we could have it back by the weekend. When I came into work, the desk sergeant called me into the office and chewed me out for not being more careful with evidence. He said the maintenance guy found a voodoo doll in the trunk of the vehicle.

I told the sergeant, "I am conscientious, and I have no idea how that got out of the evidence bag because I sealed it closed myself. Maybe someone found another one and knew where I placed the evidence in my car and dropped it off, seeing that the evidence envelope was sealed already, and when I take out the bag, I can include it in." Sergeant said, "It makes sense, but no one will own up to it because it should have been placed in a separate bag still." What can I say to the sergeant but "*Sorry*, I will be more careful." He said, "Copy."

After five hours, the maintenance man called and said, "I have no idea what to tell you, but the police vehicle is running now. We did a system check, and the car shows no error codes. The battery we installed was the old one left inside the trunk and showing fully charged. Everything checks out operational." I was surprised and said to the desk sergeant, "Maybe the doll got out of the bag on its own, and when they cleaned out the vehicle finding this doll, it seemed to be running now? How about that night you and I saw the code light bar running and there was no battery inside?" The sergeant looked at me and said, "You have a point, but leave it as is." I said, "Okay, done." From that day on, after getting the police vehicle back from the shop, it never happened again.

It will forever be one of the strangest things ever to happen to me other than that night when Dad and I heard a card game being played through the heating vent in my room and hearing Mom saying, "I won the pot." And that was a week before. Talking about being in a time tunnel movie going back to the past.

Marines Seen Entering the Cellar of a Military Apartment Complex

David A. Landry

Going through a federal or civilian police academy, you're not trained on every possible scenario that you may encounter. When assigned to your police department, things there will change for sure. You will now have to forget what you learned at the police academy and learn your department's way of doing things, and we call these changes policies. Being fully prepared to encounter everything you face will be tough. Some things your field training officer (also known as FTO), may not talk to you about will be because they had never experienced such bizarre calls their whole time on the force. Sometimes, dispatch will receive these odd calls and don't tell the responding unit in that sector all the information because of the nature of the need. Today, many people have police scanners or have an application on their cell phones to listen to all calls announced over the net.

The police are trained and required to use ten-codes to keep radio traffic or radio transmissions short and private to the civilian population. But after 9/11, ten-codes have been discontinued and straightforward language was replaced. Too many emergency teams involved, the trade center had too many problems understanding the calling unit's needs for support. Some of the departments have their own language codes. When the emergency teams were overwhelmed with the Twin Towers disasters, they used the ten-codes from their department and these caused too much confusion with the other agencies. They were using the wrong code sign when it was not an emergency but was a crisis instead.

People in public have no idea what goes through a police officer's mind when faced with a life-or-death decisions.

All it takes is a split second, which makes all the difference in who will die at that moment. What would make the public understand a police officer's role is to be placed in role-playing scenarios. This is one way they would know what decisions we have to make and how long it would take to decide. Someday, maybe this sort of class could be offered to the public free of charge, if it's not already out there. Having this class also would help show people that being a police officer is a forever thankless job, especially in today's society. There will be calls that will come in to dispatch, and they may seem to be just a simple call; but when you arrive, it's a different case. A call that may make your hair stand on your neck and arms.

Back when I was a military police officer in the Marine Corps (also known as MP), I had such a call. Or should I say my partner and I had a call from dispatch. While patrolling our zone, dispatch notified us that Marines were standing around living quarters, known as barracks or apartments, empty and ready to be torn down, and have been seen going into the cellar where the water heater room was at. When we arrived five minutes after the initial call from dispatch, there were no Marines around. We notified dispatch to verify the building number again, and we were at the right place. We called back to dispatch and informed that there were no signs of Marines hanging around the building number reported and told them that we would be going down in the cellar to the boiler room in case they were already inside.

Dispatch asked if we needed further assistance, and we declined for now and headed inside and down the stairs. In front of us was a wall of concrete. On both sides of this wall were doorways leading into the dark cellar. My partner took one side, and I took the other. Never before had my partner or I ever have gone into one of these cellars in this type of buildings. We did not know what to expect while clearing the building. We were not sure if we would meet these Marines that were supposedly there in the dark and take us on (and then that's it with both of us). I should have accepted dispatch's request for backup, but my pride got in the way and was afraid of backlash from the other police officers later, who could say, "What? You're a police officer and you're scared to do a building clearing?"

So it is what it is. We both had no choice but to clear the cellar. Going in the dark with guns drawn and slowly going around dark corners, turning on and off our flashlights to keep from being a target… *So far, so good. No contact made.* This cellar was huge. And it seemed like forever to clear it. We had to turn down our radios and go silent the whole time while making our sweep. I had no contact with my partner, and yet we were both in the same room. Having to be alone was frightening on clearing any building even in daylight, being tensed up the whole time and thinking someone anytime could jump out at you and cut your throat. I started thinking of this as soon as I entered the doorway going into the darkness.

While my partner was sweeping the other side of the room, there was no sound coming from him, not even his footsteps. So far, I had to clear five rooms on my side, and I had no idea how many more to go. The whole time while I was silently looking for marines in the dark I was sweating and very scared and the boiler room boiler was still on and generating heat for the entire building. I flashed my light all around in the room, and it was empty. I stood still and quiet to gather my thoughts. Suddenly I saw a flash of light, as if someone in that room just lit a cigarette. I slowly approached the room, and there was no way that whoever was in that room could pass me. I know what I saw, and it was a light or a match for the cigarette. I flashed my light into the room, and it was empty. I stood quiet to gather my thoughts and I said to myself *Dave stop being scared it's starting to play with your mind.*

I know it's against policy to holster your weapon during a sweep of a building, but if there was someone down there, they would have the advantage of taking my gun from my hand. If I holstered my weapon, then I'd rather fight for my life and have a chance of using my two hands and knowing my gun is still in my holster and not lost on the floor somewhere. And knowing that my partner was in the room with me, then I would not have an accidental discharge shooting at him. I continued to scan the rooms, and then I heard maybe my partner finally coming in my direction. Or was it someone else? Suddenly, I heard a sound of someone snoring coming just up in front of me, and as I was getting closer, the snoring got louder. I saw this vast tank that looked like the boiler for the entire building, and you could see a flame coming from it, showing it still being in use. Then again, I noticed that match light I saw a few minutes earlier lit again and this time, behind the tank. This time, I didn't care what happens; I was keeping my flashlight on. I scanned the whole room, and I was in the room alone, and it was the last room on my side of the sweep.

There was no way for my partner to enter this room, and this would explain why I could not hear him or his footsteps. But the snoring continued. So I walked back over to the boiler, and there was a crawl space behind it for a worker to be able to work around the tank. The snoring noise and a sound like someone was gasping for air just as they woke up came from behind it, and I thought it's so warm down there that maybe the worker decided to stay over for a bit, catch up on a nap, or overslept. Or perhaps a Marine made it a place to sleep and or hang out. Whatever it was, someone was there sleeping. As I crept inside the space of the tank and the wall, a loud sound as if someone just waking up sent my hair standing. Even with my flashlight on, I didn't see anyone there. Hearing this sound of an awaking person and not seeing this person was scaryyy. I was finally at the end of the tank, and again no one was there. It became even more frightening, not knowing where this snoring was coming from. Was it a ghost, and what about those two lights I saw that looked like a cigarette lit? What about that noise I heard earlier as if my partner was walking in the room with me? Was I again gaining my sensitivity back that I had growing up? What about my partner? Where was he the whole time? Lots of questions, no answers to any of them except for my partner's whereabouts.

As I left the boiler room and headed back out to the front door, my partner was there, and sitting smoking a cigarette. Man, I was so mad, but I didn't say a thing to him. I knew if you have nothing to say that is good, then be quiet. Trust me, and I was as quiet as a mouse. I did ask him if he heard the snoring inside he said, "No, my side was clear." I called dispatch and said the building was cleared at 7:55 p.m. "Show unit 25 back in service." Dispatch responded with repeated message. The door to the cellar was then secured with a padlock that was there, opened and hanging, and we went back into service. The whole shift,

I did not say a thing else, and my partner didn't either. As a matter of fact, he took a nap while I was patrolling our zone. Readers, you are going to love this part.

The following day, my partner and I were on patrol and a call came over the radio from the watch commander to report back to the station and meet up with him as soon as possible. When we arrived, I wondered what was so important that we had to be pulled off patrol. Could it not wait until the end of the shift? Watch commander (also known as WC) said, "Report to the Department Commander." I asked the WC what was going on. He said he was not told to discuss the matter with us. "So report to the department commander both of you now. I looked at my partner and asked him if he knew what was going on, and he said, "Your guess is as good as mine."

Going in to see the man was a big deal unless for four things: one, will get promoted; two, demoted; three, that a boy or four you messed up here is your charge for dereliction of duty. Well, I know for a fact number two and four were not happening to me. As for the other two, number one, I just got my staff sergeant, so that's off the list. The only thing left was number three. It had to be that a boy for my partner and me since we had been working together for two days. If this was, so all that I could think of was the barracks we cleared. Maybe we did such a great job clearing such a dark place by ourselves and not asking for backup or maybe get our behinds chewed out because we did not call for additional support. Man, my head was spinning from all these what-ifs. And I had all this time to think before the commander finally got both of us in.

The ultimate whatever was coming, I was ready, bring it on. Well, the time was now. The commander said, "Stay standing at attention until you answer my question. Once you answer my question, get back at attention, and you will do this until I am done with you. Clear?" We both said, "Yes, sir," together.

"Did you two receive a call from dispatch to report to a call about Marines hanging out in front of an abandoned apartment or barracks yesterday?"

We both broke the position of attention. "Yes, sir," and then went back into the position of attention.

"Did you two perform a complete building sweep?"

Both of us said, "Yes, sir."

"I will ask you once more, and if you don't answer with the correct answer, you will be demoted. Did you two perform a complete building sweep?"

I said, "Yes, sir," but my partner did not answer. I was saying to myself; I wonder if he wished he did not have that cigarette? Commander said, "Did you hear me, marine?"

My partner said, "Yes, sir."

"Are you going to answer my question? Before you answer that question, I will give you a bit of time to think very carefully before giving me your answer. Landry, describe where you entered the building and continue to the end of your search and back." I did what he asked to the end and back to the outside. Commander then looked at my partner and said, "Your turn. Tell me your beginning direction of your search to the end and back." My partner had difficulty answering his question and confessed he did not conduct his part of the sweep, and by not doing so, this has caused me to be placed into danger. I thought that this was a game to see if we did our search.

The commander said, "Great job, Landry. I am glad to see someone with *integrity* and *courage* to do what you did, *alone*. That will be all for you. Tell the WC I will be a little while with Lance Corporal S." Wow, *lance corporal* from *sergeant*. Later on that day, I saw Lance Corporal S and asked him what the heck happened back there. He told me he did not perform the search after he passed his side of the doorway because he thought he heard someone talking and got scared and came right back out. "I would go after you to tell you that maybe someone was in there, but you were already too far in, and the radio would not work in the building, and that your radio anyways was turned down. If I heard you yelling for help, I would rush in to assist you, but you were quiet, and as long as you were quiet, all would be okay until you returned. I wanted to make sure that if anyone did come out from my side where I thought I heard voices, I would detain them. But no one came out, and you returned safely. So if you knew someone was in there, even having the thought of someone being in there, why did you let me lock them in? Because I am assuming we closed someone in, correct? Did we?"

"Yes, three Marines. Someone was passing by and heard yelling from someone to let them out, and that was when dispatch got another call of the trapped men."

"Why did not say something to me the whole time we were patrolling? I thought after to go back there and let them out but being so nervous I forgot the number of the building, so I said nothing. Lance Corporal, it was a good thing that someone was going by and hearing them yelling because it would have ended tragically. Well, even though it was real people inside of the building and leaving it as a non-paranormal case. It still leaves the questions unanswered to my sweep. The loud snoring, twice lit lights as if someone were lighting a cigarette, the sound of steps in the room where there was no one there except for me. That's enough to say it was a fifty percent case. As for the Lance Corporal, he never returned for duty, and I believe he deserted the Marines.

Bizarre, right? Wait until you read the next articles.

Notes

17 Shocking and Bizarre Mysteries Of The World
That Will Send Chills Down Your Spine
(Source: http://inyminy.com/17-shocking-and-bizarre-mysteries-of-the-world-that-will-send-chills-down-your-spine/)

Bizarre Mysteries that will send chills down your spine from bizarre, gruesome murders to accidental time travelers, below is a list of high-profile mysteries that have left the world wondering and confused.

The Hinterkaifeck Murders

Call it the gruesome nature of the murders or the bizarre events that followed, and the Hinterkaifeck massacre is one of the most creepy and mysterious deaths that Germany has ever witnessed. On March 31, 1922, a family on a farm near Munich discovered murdered. A family that consisted of an elderly couple, their adult daughter with her two small children, and a new maid who had to arrive only hours before the murders took place.

The creepy part is that the previous maid had quit six months ago, was claiming the house to be haunted. The events from that day are unclear, but it appears that the family members have somehow been lured into the barn one by one, and this was where they were killed with a pickaxe. Over one hundred people were interviewed for this murder and not one single arrest. No motive ever established to explain the murders. It's hard to believe that the perpetrator(s) remained at the farm for several days – someone had fed the cattle and eaten food in the kitchen: the neighbors had also seen smoke from the chimney during the weekend. As creepy as it sounds, the killer never found.

The SS Ourang Medan Ghost Ship

You've heard about ships disappearing into the mist without a clue. Well, this ghost ship has a slightly different story to tell. SS Ourang Medan was a ship that sank in Indonesian waters, but there had been a horrible and inexplicable incident on board before it sank.

In 1947, two American vessels started receiving strange messages in Morse code from the Dutch merchant ship. The first message being – "S.O.S. from Ourang Medan we float. All officers, including the Captain, dead in chartroom and on the bridge. Probably whole crew dead."

There was something unclear following the message, but the last two words that came through were unambiguous; they were "I die." There were no messages after that. The ship that received the message approached Ourang Medan in a rescue mission but what they were about to encounter was beyond their wildest dreams. As they entered the ship, hoping to find answers and possibly some survivors. They discovered the whole crew freakishly lying around the dead (including the carcass of a dog) sprawled on their backs, the frozen faces upturned to the sun with mouths gaping open and eyes staring and their mouths open. There were no visible injuries on them. Suddenly, a fire broke out on the ship, forcing the American crew to evacuate it, exploding and sank, thus remaining a mystery forever.

The Cooper Family Falling Body

As scary as it looks, this picture has been shrouded in mystery for years now, and it is probably the most peculiar ghosts caught on camera. The story goes back to the mid-1950s taking place in Texas. The Cooper family had just moved into an old house they bought and were excited about it. They thought of preserving this memory by taking a picture of the whole family in their new home. But little did they know that there was someone else joining in on their celebration – a ghostly figure hanging upside down from the ceiling. Perhaps other stories state that an actual body did fall off from the ceiling precisely when the photograph was taken. Why does the body's face remain darkened is another mystery – a faceless body or a paranormal activity? Who knows which part is real!

The Black Knight Satellite

Legend has it that in orbit around the Earth is a mysterious, dark object which dates back perhaps 13,000 years. Its origin and purpose are a mystery to date. Dubbed the "Black Knight," this elusive satellite has allegedly been beaming strange signals towards the Earth for over 50 years, and its orbit is known to be unlike any other object orbiting the Earth. It believed that this satellite has been orbiting Earth for more than a thousand years, far longer than any space program, and its origins are not of this world.

Astronomers and scientists have calculated the satellite's weight to be over 10 tons, which would be at that time the Heaviest Artificial Satellite to orbit our Planet. However, the Ham Radio operator decoded a series of signals received from the U.F.O. Satellite. According to the decoded message, the Black Knight satellite originated from the Epsilon Bootes Star System 13.000 years ago. NASA has released official images that show the Black Knight Satellite in a clear picture, orbiting the Earth. What are the satellite's true origins, and how it got there is still a lurking mystery? Alien activity? Well, we'll leave that to you to decide.

The Villisca Axe Murders

On the evening of June 9, 1912, in Villisca, Iowa, a family of 6 went to Church. They came back around 10 pm together with two other houseguests, two girls. In the morning, their neighbors became worried when nobody from the house came out to do their usual chores. They found the door locked, but they found the whole family and the two guests bludgeoned to death in their beds upon breaking in. The killer supposedly hid in the attic and waited for them to go to sleep. Then he started with the parents to the kids and finished with the two girls in the guest room. He smashed each victim's head with an ax.

Someone also butchered the father of the family, and his eyes were missing. A terrifying detail is that nobody except one of the visiting girls was awake when they got killed. The 12-year-old girl was the only one with signs of defensive wounds on her body. Investigators thought she was awake and tried to fight back, as she was lying crosswise on the bed, and with a defensive wound on her arm. Lena's nightgown was up to her waist. She was wearing no undergarments, leading to law enforcement speculation that the killer(s) sexually molested her or attempted to do so.

There was another bizarre thing about this case; all the house mirrors were covered with bed sheets. There were several suspects, but no one was ever convicted. Many psychics believe there to be spirits dwelling in the home where his family was killed. Ghosts of the dead family? Who knows, the mystery remains unsolved to date.

The Taos Hum

In north-central New Mexico, Taos' town has been home to an unusual mystery: a resident hum of unknown origin, known as the "Taos Hum." Surprisingly, only about 2 percent of the people living in any given Hum-prone area can hear the sound.

People who've heard the Hum describe the sound as similar to a diesel engine idling nearby. And the Hum has driven virtually every one of them to the point of despair. Some describe it as a kind of torture that sometimes makes them just want to scream. It was said to be the worst at night ever. As bizarre as its nature sounds, the hum seems to have an odd effect on the sufferers – complain of headaches, nausea, dizziness, nosebleeds, and sleep disturbances. However, the buzz was heard in several areas globally, including the United Kingdom and the United States.

The buzz was first reported in the early 1990s. Several speculators believe it to be an extraterrestrial activity, beaming signals to Earth from their spaceships. Others believe it to be the result of low-frequency electromagnetic radiation, audible only to some people. Whatever be the actual cause, up to this day, no one still knows what creates such a sound, and thus the source of this hum remains shrouded in mystery.

The Voynich Manuscript

The Voynich manuscript is a notable document for its strange text that hasn't been deciphered to date. It has been written in a language that men have tried to decode to no avail through the centuries. The only idea anyone has of its origin are the drawings found on various pages. The book has been carbon-dated to the early 15th century (1404–1438). It is a handwritten book of 246 pages containing numerous illustrations and approximately 170,000 characters. The text was written from left to right, and most of the pages have illustrations or diagrams. What is unique about it? The script employed is utterly unknown and, therefore, illegible. The manuscript was named after Wilfrid Voynich, a Polish book dealer who purchased it in 1912. Not too many historical facts were known about the Voynich manuscript. It is unclear who wrote the book, what it contains, and what its purpose was. Many people have suggested different theories for deciphering the text, while some believe it's just pure nonsense and might be a hoax. But the lengths to which things have been illustrated and described through detailed pictures and texts seem highly improbable that someone would have gone through such a pain for a mere joke. Whatever it may be, the manuscript remains a confusing mystery to this day.

The Tamam Shud Case

In the early hours of December 1, 1948, an unidentified man was found dead in Somerton Beach, located in Adelaide, Australia, close to a significant Atomic Testing ground. Nothing different about it, right? But found in a secret pocket in the man's clothing was a scrap of paper with the words "Taman Shud" printed on it. The names have been translated to "finished" or "ended" based on excerpts found in The Rubaiyat of Omar Khayyam. Following a police appeal, the book was turned over to the police around the same time the body was found. A man said he found it on his car's front seat. In the book there, written was something looking like a secret code and a telephone number of a former nurse who gave a copy of The Rubaiyat to an army officer while serving in World War II. No connections have been found linking the unknown man to the nurse or the army officer.

There's been speculation over the years that the man was a spy, but none of it has been proven. Autopsy reports revealed that an unknown poison killed the man. Who was this man? Who wanted him dead? And what was the meaning of his cryptic last message? Although governments around the world have tried to identify the man, his identity remains a mystery.

DB Cooper – The Mysterious Hijacker

D. B. Cooper is a media epithet popularly used to refer to an unidentified man who hijacked a Boeing 727 aircraft in the airspace between Portland, Oregon, and Seattle, Washington, on November 24, 1971, extorted $200,000 in ransom and proceeded to jump out of the plane with a parachute. Despite an extensive search and an ongoing F.B.I. investigation, he was never found, however, and this remains the only unsolved case in U.S. aviation history.

The man was described as a business-executive type, wearing a dark suit and a black tie. While in the air, he opened his briefcase showing a bomb to the flight attendant and hijacked the plane. The plane landed in Seattle, where he demanded 200K in cash, four parachutes, and food for the crew before releasing all the passengers.

With only the pilots and one flight attendant on board, they took off from Seattle. In the 45 minutes after takeoff, Cooper sent the flight attendant to the cockpit while donning the parachute, tied the bank bag full of twenty dollar bills to himself, lowered the rear stairs, and somewhere north of Portland jumped into the night. When the plane landed with the stairs down, they found the two remaining parachutes, and on the seat, Cooper was sitting in a black-tie. Who was he and how he managed to vanish into thin air has been a mystery to date.

The Zodiac Killer

Zodiac killer is the name given to a serial killer who terrorized the San Francisco Bay Area in the late 1960s and early '70s. The self-proclaimed Zodiac Killer was directly linked to at least seven murders in Northern California in 1968 and 1969, although he claimed to be responsible for 37 victims. The Zodiac usually targeted young couples in secluded areas. He used both guns and knives as weapons. On at least one occasion, he wore an unusual costume. On two occasions, he telephoned the police afterward to report his murders.

After he taunted the police and press with his mind-boggling letters from 1969 to 1974, further communication from him abruptly stopped. Although one of the four letters was cracked, which contained an alarming message, the other three were never deciphered to date. Despite an intensive search for the killer and the investigation into numerous suspects, not a single person was never arrested for the crimes, and the case remains open.

The Dyatlov Pass Incident

On February 2, 1959, nine ski-hikers were found dead high in the Ural Mountains. This sounds like nothing unusual, considering the severe weather conditions there, but the details of the incident will make your skin crawl. Nobody knows for sure what happened since there were no survivors, but the known facts give us a horrific picture of what could have happened that night.

It all started when the hikers slit open their tent from the inside for unknown reasons and ran out. They were all experienced hikers, so this couldn't have been a mistake. They had left the tent in such a hurry that they didn't even have time to put on shoes.

The first five that were found had been frozen to death near the tent. The remaining four bodies were found only two months later. The second group of hikers were found naked and had severe injuries such as broken ribs and fractured skulls, and one woman had her eyes and tongues ripped out. Soviet authorities found no explanation. Theorists suspect paranoia, government experimentation, or that even supernatural creatures may have been involved. However, no external causes were discovered. It is still a mystery what made them break camp and run into certain death.

The Hessdalen Lights

A series of unusual lights have been reported in the Hessdalen valley, Norway, since the 1940s or earlier. Especially high activity of Hessdalen lights took place from December 1981 until the summer of 1984 when lights were observed 15–20 times per week. Since then, the movement has decreased, and now the lights are kept only 10–20 times per year. The Hessdalen light is often a bright, white, or yellow light of unknown origin standing or floating above the ground level.

These oddballs have baffled scientists for years and have even attracted attention from ufologists. They show up, gleaming around ground level, and then disappear, leaving no sign of what they are or where they came from. Whether they are ghosts sending messages from beyond or some kind of extraterrestrial signal remains a mystery.

The Solway Firth Astronaut

On a warm day in Cumbria, a man named Jim Templeton, his wife, and his daughter were picnicking on the grass above the Solway Firth. He was in a marsh taking photos of his young daughter. But little did he know that he was about to make a shocking and bizarre realization. When the man got his pictures developed, he got the chilling realization that they were not alone that sunny day. In the middle of nowhere appeared a Spaceman in full astronaut gear standing behind Jim's daughter. Except there wasn't anyone else around while they were there. Even Kodak verified that it was not tampered with. However, none of the three people had any idea that they had company. Who is this fourth person? The mystery remains unsolved.

Jack the Ripper

The name Jack the Ripper pertains to the widely popular and talked about the serial killer who thrived in the late 1800's murdering 11 women in London's east end. Most of his victims were prostitutes, whose bodies were mutilated beyond recognition, and their throats slashed. The crime scenes were a gory tableau; the brutalized bodies were perversions of the human form.

The killer was never found, but it was speculated from his murder that he was a collector who took organs as trophies. The signature of a letter that arrived during the murders gave this monster a name: Jack the Ripper. The city was whipped into a froth of suspicion and fear.

Wide dragnets snagged scores of suspects, but the police were unable to catch the killer. Vigilante committees formed, and mobs routinely chased people through the streets. And then, suddenly, the murders stopped. Despite three more years of investigation, the police never uncovered the true identity of Jack the Ripper. The unsolved case was officially closed in 1892, though interest in the killings has never dwindled.

The Black Dahlia Murder

"The Black Dahlia" was a nickname given to Elizabeth Short, an American woman who was the victim of a much-publicized murder in 1947.

Short was a 22-year-old aspiring actress who acquired the moniker of The Black Dahlia posthumously from newspapers.

On January 15, 1947, Short was found mutilated, her body sliced in half at the waist, in Leimert Park, Los Angeles, California. Short's severely mutilated body was completely severed at the waist and drained entirely of its blood. The killer had washed the body. Her face was slashed from the corners of her mouth to her ears, creating an effect called the Glasgow smile. Short also had multiple cuts on her thigh and breasts, her entire portions of her flesh sliced away.

The corpse "posed" with her hands over her head, her elbows bent at right angles, and her legs spread. Short's unsolved murder has been the source of widespread speculation, leading to many suspects; thus, no one was ever caught. Her murder happens to be one of the oldest unsolved murder cases in Los Angeles history. However, no one knew of the killer or who did the murder and the much-hyped murder mystery remains unsolved to date.

The Bizarre Death of Elisa Lam

There happen to be so many mysteries in the world, but the death of Elisa Lam is one bizarre story. In February 2013, twenty-one-year-old Elisa Lam, who stayed at the Cecil Hotel in Los Angeles, went missing for two weeks. One day, the hotel guests started complaining about a foul taste in the water. When hotel authorities investigated the matter, they found the body of Elisa Lam, naked and dead inside a covered water tank of the hotel. Autopsy reports stated that she died due to accidental drowning, and there were no traces of drugs or alcohol were found in her body. But the question remained – how did she die, and how did her body end up naked in the hotel's water tank? But that is not the creepiest part of the story. Hotel security camera footage, located above the elevator, was able to capture Elisa's last moments. But what the camera captured was beyond bizarre. The footage shows Elisa engaging in mysterious activities. She first pressed all the buttons and then proceeded to wait. But strangely, the door of the elevator did not open. Elisa went out of the elevator and started to look around but suddenly went back inside, peeking quietly through the elevator door as if she saw something or someone, and caught trying to hide from whomever she saw outside the elevator. She then suddenly started speaking and moving in fast and in a weird way. It isn't clear in the video what or whom she was talking to. After that, she suddenly proceeded to walk out of the elevator as nothing happened, and then the elevator door closed and started working again. Shortly after the elevator incident, Elisa happened to walk towards the water tank and drown herself. The creepy thing was that the hotel guests could taste and see the water's color in which Elisa's body lay dead. The mystery remains unsolved and mysterious to date.

The Accidental Time Traveler

Rudolph Fentz is a known accidental time traveler.

Believe it or not, Rudolph lived in New York City and disappeared without a clue on Sunday, August 27, 1876.

The twenty nine-year-old had left home after dinner to go for an evening stroll only never to return. At the time, alone drunk claimed he saw Rudolph disappear as he crossed a street in Times Square known as Long Acre Square. One second he was there, and the next, he just vanished in the blink of an eye. The witness was discounted due to being a known drunk, and Rudolph's family reported him missing.

But, in 1950, a man with mutton chop sideburns and Victorian-era duds popped up in Times Square. Witnesses said he looked startled, and then a minute later, he was hit by a car and killed. Officials in the morgue searched his entire body and found items in his pockets that were not of this period.

A copper token for a beer worth five cents, bearing the name of a saloon, which was unknown, even to older residents of the area, A bill for the care of a horse and the washing of a carriage, drawn by a delivery stable on Lexington Avenue that was not listed in any address book. About seventy dollars in old banknotes, Business cards with the name Rudolph Fentz and an address on Fifth Avenue. Surprisingly, none of these objects found on the dead man showed any signs of aging.

NYPD tried using this information to identify the man.

But found that Fifth Avenue's address was part of a business; its current owner did not know Rudolph Fentz. Fentz's name was not listed in the address book; his fingerprints were not recorded anywhere. The investigation continued, and finally, Rudolph Fentz Jr. was in a telephone book of 1939. Upon contact with the bank, Fentz Jr. died five years before, but his widow was still alive but lived in Florida. Upon contacting her, the NYPD learned that her husband's father had disappeared in 1876, aged twenty nine.

He had left the house for an evening walk but never returned. Accidental time travel or something out of the paranormal? We'll leave that to you to decide.

*****

You think this was bizarre, what until you read the next section.

Imagine What Dead Bodies Can Do
Source: http://inyminy.com/10-spine-chilling-things-you-never-imagined-dead-bodies-can-do/

When a person dies, their body undergoes a series of changes, from stiffening muscles to loss of color and fluids. While we may have seen some of these things being portrayed on real crime TV shows, others seem almost unbelievable and quite possibly horrifying when one learns about them.

Make Noises

While corpses do not necessarily scream or yell, there have been instances where dead bodies have indeed moaned, groaned, hissed, and even grunted.

The reason behind these noises is that the air and gases produced in the body before death are still left inside, and they require an escape. So, air released from a cadaver's windpipe vibrates the vocal cords causing the body to make noises that resemble a grunt or a moan. Similarly, gastric gases make noises similar to a hiss as the gases escape through the intestines.

Exploding Bodies

You might've heard stories of bodies exploding from the inside out. Though most of them not exaggerated, they might not be too far from reality as well.

Sometime in January 2013, a corpse exploded in a mausoleum in Melbourne. Those present at this time of the incident were traumatized for weeks by the event. What happens is, as the body starts to decompose, the gases created as a result begin to build up, and they require a means of escape. If they fail to release, the continuous buildup may cause the body to "explode."

Other explanations include phenomena such as spontaneous human combustion. But the possibility of the body combusting or exploding is relatively low. After death, the body temperature starts to increase, which could be due to drugs, trauma, or even brain signals. But the temperature does go down as the corpse goes through various stages of decomposition.

Elimination of Excretions

When a body dies, the muscles inside undergo relaxation, including the sphincter muscles, which control the release of bodily fluids like urine or feces. After death, these muscles no longer receive signals from the brain to remain contracted; thus, contents left in the body are eliminated.

Whether the urine or feces are released or not highly depends on how you die. For instance, people who were ill for a prolonged period don't possess many excretions as they're usually known to lose their appetites or eat lesser than they usually would. However, if the death is sudden, whatever was in the body is eliminated forcefully and sometimes immediately.

Giving Birth after Death

Unfortunately, death doesn't have a moral compass, so women who were pregnant at the time of their death might experience what is known as postmortem birth.

While giving birth may be the most beautiful and memorable experience in a woman's life, giving birth after dying happens to be an opposite experience, especially for those who have to deal with the corpse. Also known as coffin births, there have been numerous incidents of finding a newborn near a dead body in a morgue or sometimes even on the grave.

The pressure of the gases built up in the body after death causes the fetus to expel out. While such cases were common in ancient times due to a lack of medical science advances, they continue to happen. In January 2018, people were shocked to find a fetus in the coffin of a woman in South Africa who died ten days earlier.

Dead Bodies Still Move after Death

Tales of dead bodies sitting up straight have been told a lot throughout the years, but the possibility of it happening is slim to none. The body can, however, make small movements after death. The moves might not be outrageous but can startle people working around the body.

Corpses have been known to twitch or shift, even clench muscles, primarily because after death, the body's muscles are still receiving nerve signals, causing the body to contract and relax even after death. Once the calls stop transporting to the muscles, the cadaver makes its final movements visible in the form of fingers moving, toes wiggling and muscles twitching.

Another factor that may cause such movements is how the person died. For instance, sudden deaths, even events such as electrocution, may cause actions in the body.

Appear to Grow Even after Death

In the past, people have claimed that even after death, the corpse continued to grow hair and nails. As bizarre as it sounds, such growth seen in a corpse is merely an illusion. What appears to be growing is caused due to dehydration experienced by the body due to death. This dehydration causes the skin around the nails and hair to retract (pull back), which gives the illusion of longer nails and hair. Goosebumps after death also impact how the hair looks on a dead body. This is why morticians tend to apply moisturizer on bodies to hydrate the dry skin of the cadaver.

Look Aroused Even When You're Dead

While it may be embarrassing to get aroused at the wrong moment in life, getting an erection after death is creepy as hell. When a body dies, the blood previously circulating uniformly through the body starts to pool in the body's lower sections. If the death occurred due to a spinal injury, or when the person was face-down, the likelihood of the blood collecting in the genital areas increases. This continuous blood pool causes the dead man's penis to react, a phenomenon more commonly known as priapism. While this is more common in men, women can also be seen where their labia become enlarged, causing the clitoris to swell in size.

Know They're Dead For Sure

There have been numerous stories of people "coming back from the dead." While these experiences of what they call 'afterlife' may be different from each other, scientists might have an explanation for them. After dying, the brain can retain some element of consciousness or awareness. One study showed that of the 2060 cardiac arrest survivors observed in a study, legally declared dead, around 40% of them reported to have been fully aware of their surroundings and conversations going around them. This period of awareness is, however, short-lived. There is a mere 20-30 seconds of awareness time available to the body. In cases of decapitation, the severed head still produces EEG waves even after death. However, scientists believe that these limited seconds of awareness lead the body into unconsciousness. Still, the idea of being aware that you are dead, for a, however short amount of time, is terrifying.

Experience Pain Is Highly Possible

The people who donate their organs, there is a crucial time limit in which the organs need extraction from the dead body. However, scientists have started to fear that even after the brain has died, the body still experiences pain after death. Many dead bodies have found to exhibit various reactions when they are cut open to retrieve the organs, rise in blood pressure, twitching, and body movements being among the few. Research says that the brain can stay alive for up to 10 minutes after being declared brain-dead, which means that it is highly likely that the body can experience pain signals that are still being sent by the brain to the body. That is why many people have opted for anesthesia after death in case the pain thing is real. Bone-chilling!

Yes, Dead Bodies Can Still Orgasm after Death

Yes, you heard that right, dead bodies can orgasm after death. But, for bodies that no longer have oxygen circulating within them, this is not the case. For clinically dead bodies, meaning, the bodies that are kept alive for organ donations, doctors who work with such bodies sometimes electrically stimulate parts of the spine. This stimulation activates a reflexive action in the autonomous nervous system, which can cause an orgasm. But since the bodies are clinically dead, there is no real pleasure from this experience. The reflex is purely out of the brain, still sending signals to the body.

Notes

Mr. Bryan Chocoteco

Biography

Soon to graduate from Fallbrook High School in 2021 at the age of eighteen and desiring to be the next *Chesty Puller*, the most decorated Marine in the United States Marines Corps.

2017–2021: ROTC, reached the rank of sergeant major, credited to hard work and dedication. Assists CO and XO by over watching platoon sergeants in their daily operations.

2019–2019: In July joined the Devil Pups, a ten-day actual USMC boot camp course.

2019–2019: JROTC Raiders Competition, competed against fifteen other all-service units; came in second place.

2020–2021 ROTC Drill Team, ROTC Fitness Instructor, ROTC Color Guard, ROTC Rifleman.

High school GPA: 4.0

Bryan's desire is to be assigned to a Fleet Anti-terrorism Security Team (FAST) or to a Marine Security Guard unit and serve Embassy Duty anywhere overseas. Bryan left for Marine Corps boot camp in San Diego, California, on June 6, 2021 and is coming out of boot camp as an E-2 Private First Class.

Volunteer for St. Peter the Apostle Catholic Church in Fallbrook, California, Bryan has traveled to Ethiopia as a missionary for Unforgotten Faces and teaching the Bible to Ethiopian children and adults.

A Hotel Worshiping and a Visit from Santa Muerte

Bryan Chocoteco

Addis Ababa, also spelled *Addis Abeba*, is the capital and largest city of Ethiopia. It is located on a well-watered plateau surrounded by hills and mountains, in the geographic center of the country.

Kimberly Zember founder of Unforgotten Faces has found Addis Ababa to be a safe place to worshiping the word of God. Addis Ababa is a beautiful and friendly place for people to become missionaries and an excellent place to perform humanitarian services. Ethiopia is a place where your faith may be tested as well. I was there for ten days—everything was terrific, and we all got along so well with the people there and with each other.

We were midway through our retreat, and the plan of this day was a prayer-worship gathering at the hotel. The group consisted of around eight to ten people for this one afternoon. All of us sat on the floor and were instructed to close our eyes while we prayed. While I had my eyes closed and began to pray along with the others, suddenly, Santa Muerte materialized right before me. Muerte was looking directly at me and in silence, with its blade in its right hand. I was frozen and had no idea why Muerte was in my thoughts at this time. She was looking at me, and with her left hand, she was pointing her finger at me.

I yelled out and asked, "What do you want, and why are you pointing at me?" Muerte just stood there in silence. I said three times, "In Jesus's name! In Jesus's name! In Jesus's name!" Suddenly, Muerte raised its left hand, palm facing me, and this was when I felt my body moving away from Muerte and moving back towards the edge of the porch that had a drop of at least twenty to thirty feet below and landing on top of trees and rocks. As I was going over the edge of the porch, my arms were swaying all over the place. I was trying to catch something to stop me from hitting the trees or ground on the way down. Suddenly, something grabbed my hands to keep me from falling, and I was back with my group in prayer worshiping.

I sat there in disbelief of what just happened and thinking, *Did I fall asleep, or did I experience something supernatural?* I guess I will never know, but it was so real. I said nothing to no one at that moment because I was still trying to calm down from this incident. But one thing was for sure, by saying "In Jesus's name!" three times, it had upset Santa Muerte so much that Muerte continued to push me over the edge of the porch. I believe Jesus was the one who caught me from falling and brought me back to the safety of my group of worshipers. I want to say to Jesus, "Thank you and trusting me in believing in you and that my faith was tested today. Have I proven to you to be genuine and sincere, Jesus?"

Later after the meeting, I confronted two older people in my group and told them of my experience, and they said it sent chills up their spines and hair standing on their arms. This was my first experience of a bizarre moment, and I am sure it won't be my last time.

https://www.wallpapersin4k.org/images/598247

Who Is Santa Muerte?

Nuestra Señora de la Santa Muerte, often shortened to Santa Muerte, is an idol, female deity or folk saint in Mexican and Mexican-American folk Catholicism. A personification of death, she is associated with healing, protection, and safe delivery to the afterlife by her devotees.

7 Things to Know about La Santa Muerte, Mexico's Folk Saint of Death
Source: https://www.huffpost.com/
entry/7-things-to-know-about-la_b_8385476

The Mexican folk saint of death—an intimidating skeletal figure holding a scythe—goes by many names, most notably La Santa Muerte. Though worship of **La Santa Muerte** has become inextricably intertwined with drug cartels, she has become an all-purpose deity for working-class and poor Mexicans, not just criminals. As veneration for Santa Muerte grows, so do the misconceptions about what she represents.

1. La Santa Muerte has dark roots. However, some believe the folk saint emerged as a combination of Spanish Catholicism and Aztec worship of Mictecacihuatl, the underworld's queen, and the afterlife.

Before 2001, devotees of Santa Muerte primarily worshiped in private, erecting shrines in their closets or personal spaces. In recent years, adulation has spread like wildfire—mostly since **Enriqueta Romero**, better known as **Doña Queta**, erected a life-size statue of the saint on the sidewalk outside of her home in Tepito, an impoverished, crime-riddled barrio of Mexico City. Doña Queta, along with **Enriqueta Vargas**, has become the two most prominent leaders of the Santa Muerte movement in Mexico. When Vargas's son was murdered in 2008, she inherited his seventy-five-foot, fiberglass Santa Muerte statue, and temple. Today, worshipers flock to the temple in Tultitlán, where Vargas performs weddings and baptisms.

2. While Catholicism rates continue to decline across Latin America, the number of La Santa Muerte devotees continues to surge.

In an interview with *Vice*, R. Andrew Chesnut, the author of *Devoted to Death: Santa Muerte, the Skeleton Saint*, said that the folk saint boasts between ten and twelve million devotees. However, La Santa Muerte doesn't demand exclusive devotion. Many followers also practice other religions, such as Catholicism.

3. Don't let her name confuse you; the Catholic Church has not canonized or approved La Santa Muerte.

The Church continues to wage war on what they perceive to be a "celebration of devastation and hell." In 2013, Gianfranco Ravasi, the president of the Vatican's Pontifical Council for Culture, gave an impassioned statement about the folk saint. "It's not religion just because it's dressed up like religion," he said. "It's a blasphemy against religion. Everyone is needed to put the brakes on this phenomenon, including families, churches, and society."

4. Many—though certainly not all—of La Santa Muerte's devotees live on the margins of society.

They are poor, disenfranchised, or criminals. "After all, the very origins of the public cult are tied to crime," wrote Chestnut in Devotion To Death. "Doña Queta's life-size effigy of the saint, which is the object of devotion to tens of thousands of chilangos (a slang term for residents of Mexico City), was a gift to her from one of her sons to thank the Powerful Lady for his speedy release from prison." In a nod to La Santa Muerte's criminal following, the saint made an infamous cameo on Breaking Bad. In an eerie scene at the beginning of the third season, two hitmen for the Juárez Cartel—called The Cousins—pay tribute to a statue of La Santa Muerte, and ask her for the death of Heisenberg. Like death, La Santa Muerte does not discriminate; everyone—rich, poor, or somewhere in between—will die, and La Santa Muerta will listen to the prayers of them all as well.

5. Some devotees believe that cutting a deal with La Santa Muerte can be a double-edged sword.

In interviews with the Houston Press, several followers said that you must make a promise if you ask La Santa Muerte for a favor. If you don't keep that promise, she can take away a loved one.

6. Many of the rituals involved in the worship of La Santa Muerte mimic Catholic customs.

People use rosaries, candles, and prayers in their worship, and you can hardly deny her eerie physical similarity to la Virgen de Guadalupe. However, many find themselves drawn to La Santa Muerta because of her non-judgmental nature, a stark contrast to the attitude often presented by the Catholic Church.

7. Perhaps because La Santa Muerte exists outside the confines of the Catholic Church, many followers feel more comfortable asking her for less useful favors, such as protection over a shipment of drugs.

However, she grants all kinds of requests—not just the criminal ones. To ask for a favor, followers should pray to her consistently, act with gratitude, and present an offering, such as fruit, flowers, cigars, incense, food, or alcohol, in exchange for the request.

Unforgotten Faces

My worshiping group was with Unforgotten Faces. This is a nonprofit organization providing school materials, clothing, food, and money to help build schools, etc. Unforgotten Faces is headed by Kimberly Zember, founder, and has been successful for many years.

https://www.unforgottenfaces.org/ Accepting Donations

Who We Are

Everything we do is fueled by the love of God, allowing us to reach a hungry and hurting world.

Our Mission

The focus of Unforgotten Faces is to seek God first so that all we do brings Him honor and glory. Set on a Christian Foundation we live operating in the Gospel of Jesus Christ through lives devoted to Him. The fruit of our work is shown through education, Health care, feeding programs, development, outreach, mission, and training.

In **Addis Ababa,** Ethiopia Unforgotten Faces is a CA registered 501(c)3 non-profit organization serving in Ethiopia. UF provides for over 270 children through a variety of different programs we have created. Our focus is support and education for children who have lost one or both of their parents. We provide meals five days a week, school fees, necessary educational materials as well as training and tutoring and medical care. Equally important is the work we do with the children's parents, training them in business and development skills as well as other important life skills training throughout the year all helping them work towards self-sustainability.

Kim Zember

Kim Zember, UF founder
https://www.unforgottenfaces.org/

Unforgotten Faces believes that all children deserve a healthy life and a bright future.

Unforgotten Faces has seen that daily meals, medical care, a solid educational foundation while having the sense of belonging, helps lead children towards a full life. We aim to meet all of our children's needs while striving to show them Jesus' love.

UF trusts that in all that we do, the children have the chance to grow up with the opportunity to follow the vision God has put in their hearts, leading them to be positive influences within their country and wherever God may lead them.

https://www.youtube.com/watch?v=pJWEgjUSjdA Aug 7, 2008
https://www.youtube.com/watch?v=R2Byyk6YfLM March 1, 2019
Donations are always welcomed.

Dr. Leggie [Leh 'jee] L. Boone

Biography

My name is Dr. Leggie [Leh 'jee] Boone, and I am a forensic analyst for a sheriff's office in Florida. I have been involved in forensic sciences since 1993, including overlapping years as a crime scene investigator and educator in Baltimore, Maryland. Crime Scene Investigation found me shortly after completing my bachelor's degree in biology, while I worked toward my initial journey: veterinary science. As a civilian investigator, I learned my city, law enforcement family, and self-reliance in coping with the tragedies of criminal violations daily.

Sometimes, my decompression method include writing songs, writing poetry, or dreaming graphically detailed dreams and journaling them. When my daughter was born, I left the hectic schedule of being a forensic services supervisor, pharmacy assistant, and adjunct professor to teach full-time. Teaching high school and college sciences inspired the pursuit of my master's degree in forensic science. In 2008, I moved to Florida, where I returned to crime scenes, and I was recruited to become a forensic analyst by my current agency. I have also been active in my community through my Zeta Phi Beta Sorority, Inc. membership, and affiliation with multiple civic organizations.

I attained my Ph.D. and master of philosophy in public policy and administration in criminal justice, intending to improve policies and curricula in collegiate forensic sciences and law enforcement agency and crime scene investigation training. I am still dreaming vividly through it all, with plans to produce volumes for interpretation, enlightenment, or entertainment. I am inspired by my mother's and daughter's constant support, both named Leggie, and I am driven by my faith to be an author, a leader, and an agent of social change.

If you want to contact Dr. Leggie [Leh 'jee] Boone for comments write to LLBoone12@gmail.com.

Hugged a Murderer

Dr. Leggie [Leh 'jee] L. Boone

Poem 1

I met two little boys, just one week before
I assisted with a shooting, that had happened right next door
They watched me from their stroller while they ate their snack
They caught my eye, I smiled and waved,
and the little one smiled back
They both were small and dirty, they were curious but meek
While I worked, the thought came and
went as to why they didn't speak
I brushed the thought away and got back to my scene
I took notes and pictures, measured, drew, and everything in between
The Guardian had mentioned puppies and my heart just gave in
Babies and puppies at the same time, plus it was butterfly season
She brought out three of the cutest things, just a few days old,
Of the eight born, seven survived and six had already been pre-sold
With help from the willing detectives, I
collected the last of the evidence
We packed everything, gave another once-over
and someone asked just one more question.
The witnesses volunteered info, the subjects
had touched their possessions
I rolled their fingerprints and collected DNA,
for the purpose of elimination
I said my goodbyes having had a good day
and headed back to the P.D.

Just one week later, I had to return in
reference to the death of the baby.
I went to the hospital first. EMS brought the injured child here
The little boy's body went limp and he died,
and I waited as I held back a tear
You can never cry at a crime scene. It's not
written but it's best to stay neutral
Never get too attached to the victim. It reduces
your ability to remain impartial.
But we always hurt for the young, the most
innocent of God's children
I'll save my tears for when I get home, as I
wondered what happened to him.
Upon returning to the house I had been to
before, I hugged the Guardian there
She appreciated my gesture and smiled a half-
smile as I left her to begin my scene care
I attended all secondary scenes, as well as the pathologist's dissection
The family had lied about the circumstances of his
death, his injuries and their efforts to save him
The baby boy died of a broken heart, the muscle
torn by great force from a blow
He had bruises all over, a few abrasions as well,
and the bite-marks at first didn't show
Child abuse from a bi-polar keeper, someone entrusted with his care
Her own loses had damaged her capacity to turn
off the hate she confused with despair
We now know that she needed counseling;
the children needed alternate means
She'll be in jail getting mental health care while
the baby boy has become a memory.
Maybe she needed my hug. Maybe I needed to
share To give positively to a negative thing, when
all we needed was to be made aware
Death Investigation of a Two-Year Old, 2012, Winter Haven

My First Last Call

Dr. Leggie [Leh 'jee] L. Boone

Poem 2

The baby lay on the hospital bed with tubes and gauze with tape
The little one lay still and quiet, with no one there but me
I had asked my questions from the police now waiting just outside
The curtains drawn left me alone to quickly do my job
I wrote some notes and got some gloves to do what I had to do
I took lots of pictures, some with a scale, then came the time to move
I lifted an arm, limp and light, to reveal multiple contusions
I lifted a leg to see the same in patterned purple bruises
I stepped out to get a nurse to point out more of the damage
She showed me the x-ray of the fractured skull,
the result of one man's rampage
The culprit said the baby fell down, but we all knew better
The fall would have been from two stories
or more to get this badly injured
He had beaten this child for crying and
shook hard when that didn't stop
He had slammed the baby onto the floor,
picked her up and then he dropped
He treated her not like a person, who deserved
much more than he could give
Her voice is silenced forever, she's brain dead and her body won't live.
This child, like too many others, was left in the wrong hands
No value for life, yet he claimed love for his wife,
who had this child by some other man

This happened before they came together but still he harbored disgust
Entrusted with her care, he lacked willingness to
share love for this kid who cried too much
I left this scene feeling heavy. As a mother, they all look like mine
Small and fragile, broken and bruised, the trauma effects their minds
Those that live through it are troubled, and
many troubled have difficult lives
Lives of abuse, not recognizing love, needing
something they can't seem to find
Some can get strength from others, counseled, encouraged by faith
Life is a gift, not to be taken, but shared
to help others before it's too late
Death comes too soon for too many, in life
they're just starting to crawl
But pain is an un-breaking cycle, once transferred its felt by us all.
Once in my car I let go of the dam holding back silent tears
I prayed for the baby, the family and perp,
that their pain would soon disappear
I decided that this scene was it- I needed to leave this today
No more bodies, and no more crime scenes and
no strangers in the height of their pain
I had somehow made their blues mine, leaving
scene after scene feeling hopeless
It's hard to feel nothing, be neutral, when
the impact of crime pulls me in.
The next day I turned in my letter and decided to step out on faith
To learn more and teach allowed me to release
all the stories of others' despair.
Child Death as a result of Abuse, 2002

Notes

Mr. Prashant Singh

Biography

Prashant grew up in Bahrain, where he pursued his schooling in science. After completing his education, he currently graduated with B.Sc.(H) forensic science from Amity University Haryana. He is pursuing his M.Sc. toxicology from National Forensic Science University, Ministry of Home Affairs, Gujarat.

He is a research enthusiast, and he aims to build a definite awareness of scientific knowledge in society. He has participated in many National and International Conferences and has even won prizes in a few. He is also a part-time social worker who works for the Education of Underprivileged Students. He has undertaken many projects in his field.

Prashant is also a writer; he has written various articles and papers related to the current interest and scientific knowledge for various national and international magazines and platforms. He writes to help society understand the subject matter in his articles in a simple yet informative manner.

He has also done many certification courses from reputed institutions like West Virginia University, Kings College London, the University of Sheffield, etc., to enhance his knowledge in his fields of interest. He is also currently founder of a student initiative-based website, The Forensic Corner, that is working to aware the society about forensic sciences and its related fields.

The Ghost with a Scientific Temperament

Prashant Singh

The Aravalli Range is famous for its mountain range that spreads across the northwest regions of India. This beautiful range has a lot of big and small lakes nearby, enhancing its beauty. The majestic appearance of this range has attracted many people. But it has been said that beautiful things often have a dark side. For a while now, there have been many crimes ongoing near this region, so to help solve these crimes, a forensic laboratory was built near this range to assist the police in their investigations.

Creepy stories have been circulated about this laboratory. It has been said that the building where this lab was built was earlier a mental asylum; some even say it was built on a graveyard, "I think you shouldn't join them, Raj," said Meena. "Meena, you don't have to worry. It's all rubbish. It's probably to scare the criminals," said Raj. "But can't you wait to join elsewhere?" asked Meena. "Meena, we just got married, and you know this is my first job. We have to manage our expenses. There is nothing to worry about, I promise," said Raj, kissing her on her forehead.

It was Monday morning, and Raj, a forensic expert, was getting ready to go to his new job.

Meena, Raj's wife, was packing his breakfast to go; she accidentally dropped a glass plate on the floor and started to cry. Raj rushed into the kitchen and said, "It's okay, dear. Why are you crying over a broken plate?"

"Raj, you know a broken glass is a sign of bad luck. I am distraught for you," said Meena crying. Raj comforted her and said, "Don't be superstitious. It's all rubbish. Science doesn't permit us to believe in such hoax." Soon they both left their apartment. Raj dropped Meena off at the university, where she was an assistant professor of forensic science. He headed toward the forensic laboratory where he would be working.

Raj soon arrived at lane number 13, where he saw a signboard saying "Forensic laboratory No. 666 ahead." He arrived at the main entrance; the surrounding atmosphere was arid and lonely; a thick fog covered half the area nearby, and the Aravalli Range could be seen from a distance. Not a was sound heard, and the only life that could be seen was that of the lab personnel. The lab was new, and its location, typically far away from the lab workforce, was significantly less than its size. Raj parked his car and entered the lab at 9:00 a.m. The guard on duty checked his personnel log and gave him entry and was then welcomed in the lab by Dr. Kohli, who was in charge of the lab.

Dr. Kohli was a middle-aged man. He was a narcotics expert and had a shiny blue pen in his coat pocket with the letter K carved on it. "I hope you didn't find any difficulties on your way," said Dr. Kohli, smiling.

"No, sir, I didn't, though the lab's location does surprise me," said Raj.

"Yes, I agree," replied Dr. Kohli. At 9:00 a.m., the two men walked through the narrow hallway of the ground floor, passing the ballistics lab, serology and fingerprints lab, followed by the mortuary. They then took the lift to the first floor where Dr. Kohli had his office. There they both sat and started to complete the final particulars of his job.

"Raj, what made you choose forensic science as a career?" asked Dr. Kohli.

"I have always been fascinated by the wide multidisciplinary approach this field had, the application of basic sciences and its wide range of research opportunities made me pursue this as a career."

"Interesting, so why did you choose forensic medicine and toxicology as specialization in particular?"

"Sir, I believe the dead body and its related parts always have something to say that can help us find the cause and manner of death; that was the main reason I got my specialization in this subject."

"Great, I like your enthusiasm. I would love to see you start working as soon as possible for me. Your lab and office are on the third floor. You can go there right away," said Dr. Kohli.

Dr. Kohli handed Raj his ID card and a lab coat and told him that the case files and other required tools would be in the lab. In a cold voice to Raj, he also mentioned that he is the only person on the third floor. "If you need anything, my number and the other members mentioned are on the third-floor wall."

Raj arrived on the third floor, and it was very lonely; there was not a sound to be heard. He decided to explore the floor. The first room was his lab and office, the second room on the floor was a record room, and the last two rooms, very shabby and dusty, were locked from the outside and had some holy symbol on it. It was creepy at the sight, but Raj decided not to give much thought and returned to his lab to start his work assigned.

When he entered his lab, he saw a table with a small lamp on it with a few files. Beside the table, there was a wide-open hall-like area where chemicals and other equipment were stored. Without wasting much time, he hung his coat on his revolving chair, sat, and started reading his first case.

The case read as follows: "Body recovered at the shore of a lonely lake, suspected of poisoning the queries from the police said, poisoning is the cause of death? If yes, what poison?" Raj was very excited to work on his first case. Before examining the viscera (materials retained from the body after an autopsy that can be checked in a lab for poisons, drugs, etc.), Raj decided to go to the mortuary to have a look at the corpse to understand what might be the cause of death.

Raj took the lift and made his way to the mortuary where he met Dr. Robin, a very old-looking man who looked rude.

"Who are you? And what brings you here?" asked Dr. Robin.

"I am the new forensic expert on the third floor, and I came here to see the body of the victim of case number 12," answered Raj.

Dr. Robin stared at him, gave a stern look, then said, "The register is on the table. Make your entry and follow me," said Dr. Robin.

They soon entered the mortuary, which was very cold, about 4° C. This temperature was maintained to preserve the bodies. Raj then soon saw the body of the victim; it was green and was a bit bloated. This indicated that the body was around three to four days old, and the nails and hair of the victim had white traces. It was an indication that it might be a case of arsenic poisoning.

He soon left and returned to his lab; it was already 2:00 p.m. He took a skin sample and subjected it to a preliminary examination followed by a confirmatory test using IR and other complex instruments. The pieces indeed had traces of arsenic.

He recorded his findings and sat to write the report of his analysis. Suddenly, he heard the laughter of a woman in the corridor. He rushed outside and saw no one there. It was very odd; he came into his lab a bit frightened. He drank some water and started to work again. By 5:00 p.m., he was finished and most of the staff had begun to leave. He packed his stuff, shut off all the lights, and then locked the lab door. As he was just about to leave, he heard a loud thud at the door's last room, and he turned around—there was no one there. That sound felt as if someone pushed that door from inside. He walked towards the door, but again, there was no one there. As he was looking at the lock, he heard the voice of Dr. Kohli, who shouted, "Raj, what are you doing there? Let's go. It's already 6:30 p.m." Raj walked away from the door and toward Dr. Kohli. As they were leaving, Raj said to Dr. Kohli, "What's in those locked rooms? And today, I felt like as if someone was inside that room."

There was silence, and the look on the face of Dr. Kohli was cold; it appeared as if he was hiding something. "There's nothing in those rooms, it's just new labs, and the sound you heard was probably of the rats. There's nothing to worry about." Then the two men left the lab.

That evening, Raj couldn't stop thinking about what he heard earlier today. He had gone to pick Meena, and they soon left and reached home. "So, how was your day?" asked Meena. "It was great," answered Raj.

Both had their dinner and then gone to bed for the night. Around 1:37 a.m., Raj was sweating in his sleep. Raj saw a woman near the locked door. She was standing with her head leaning on the wall; her long hair covered her face, the reason why Raj wasn't able to see her face. Her red dress was dusty and torn in some places. She was murmuring something, but it was not clear as to what she was saying.

The hallway of the third floor appeared long and dark. Raj called out, "Hey, who are you? What are you doing here?" But there was no answer from her. Raj started to walk toward her slowly. While he was frightened, still, he continued moving toward her. When he reached her, the woman stopped murmuring, and she started to cry. Raj moved his right hand toward that woman. She turned toward him and shouted. She had burning red eyes, her face was blistered and had many scars, her hair turned gray. Raj nearly fainted and was frightened to his wits.

"It's probably just a bad dream. Come sleep," said Raj's wife, Meena.

Raj drank some water and went back to sleep. Raj awakened to sounds again, saw the same woman; this time, she walked inside the record room. He followed her and entered the record room behind her. There was no one there but a file that was lying there on the table. The door started closing behind me, and when he had gone over to look at that file, it appeared to be an old case. Raj opened the file, and in there was a photo of a woman who was burned to death. When the case was taken to court, the case was determined closed due to lack of evidence. The woman in the pictures appeared to be the one he saw by the door in the hallway.

As Raj turned around, there was blood all over the walls, and it stated "Justice!" Suddenly, Raj woke up again from a deep sleep. The rest of the night, Raj couldn't fall back to sleep. He was frightened and confused, wondering if this was a dream or if it was real. The next day, he went to his lab, still thinking about what he saw in his dream and wondering why he was dreaming of this dream.

Raj could not concentrate on his work, and the thoughts of this woman just kept on bothering him. Suddenly, he decided to go to the record room to search for that file he saw in his dream.

That whole morning, Raj searched the record room, and he came across a similar-looking file; and when he opened it, there she was the photo of that dead woman. He took this file and returned to his lab to review it.

The case was about a forensic expert who was killed in a fire that consumed the lab. It seemed like an accident, but there wasn't sufficient information. Something was fishy. The photos in the file appeared to be from the third floor. Raj said to himself, "Dr. Kohli never mentioned anything to me about this fire. Why is this?"

Raj had a feeling that it had something to do with the two locked rooms. He decided to break the two locks and find out for himself. He took some acid from his lab and, using a dropper, slowly dropped some of the acid on the safety locks. Raj opened the first locked room, and the door made a very rusty sound. Raj searched around for the light switch and turned on the lights.

He was frightened at what he saw. The room was very dull and shabby and burned from the fire. That room appeared to be a psychologist's office, and then he started to look around and saw some unburnt files, remaining chemical bottles, and so on. Raj opened the table's drawer and saw a photo of a young lady he saw in his dreams. He decided to open the last room's door using the same method as he did for the first door.

That door had some strange holy symbol written on it, but Raj ignored it and removed the lock. As soon as he opened the door to that room, a cold breeze had passed through him. He tried to turn on the lights, but the light switch did not work. He took out his cell phone, and with the dim light on his phone, he started moving in the room. Once again, as did the first door, it closed behind him. He was now trapped inside.

As he was looking around, he bumped onto a table and dropped his phone. When he picked up his phone, lights were showing on the floor, and he was terrified, not knowing where the lights were coming from. Suddenly, there was a shape of a woman's structure lit on the floor as if it were luminol, which detects blood patterns. It was where the woman was found dead—from the photos. Raj panicked and ran toward the door, but the door wouldn't open. He was terrified at what he was seeing and was trapped with nowhere else to go.

Suddenly, the lights came on in the room; he was watching the dead woman running around in the place he was in, and Dr. Kohli was catching her and then restraining her to a chair. The doctor began injecting some chemicals into her neck, and she was screaming out loud. It appeared that the doctor was experimenting.

Raj thought that he was hallucinating, but seeing this event in the past as it happened, suddenly, everything vanished, and he was back in the dark room again. It was a creepy experience. Right after the door opened on its own, Raj got out of there and went back to the lab. Raj was frightened and very confused as to what he just witnessed. He kept what he had encountered to himself and started to carry out his assignment as hired.

Raj saw that woman in his dream again, and this time, Dr. Kohli was now in the room he opened first, and Raj saw the doctor abusing her. After seeing this in his dream, he woke up. Raj looked at the time.

Raj decided to read more about Dr. Kohli and found a few news articles about the lab. He discovered that Dr. Kohli used to work in this building before it became a lab. It was a mental asylum, and Raj knew that Dr. Kohli had something to do with the case. He went to his office and asked him, "Why, didn't you tell me this used to be an asylum? Who knows how many died in this building? What happened here, Dr. Kohli?"

Dr. Kohli gave him the cold and dreadful look and said, "What do you know, Raj?"

"I think you're involved somehow in all these paranormal activities that I have been witnessing lately," said Raj.

"There was an accident here due to a small short circuit in a heater, and we lost one of our experts in the fire. That's in the past, and it shouldn't be any concern to you," shouted Dr. Kohli.

"How did she die, Dr. Kohli?" Raj asked.

"A short circuit caused it, I said."

Raj told Dr. Kohli that he saw the case file. "And it says the case is closed due to a lack of evidence."

"You saw what!" shouted Dr. Kohli. "You have opened the closed rooms. You shouldn't have done that," moaned Dr. Kohli.

Raj returned to the third floor, and he could hear a woman crying from his lab. He rushed to the lab to find no one there. And he saw a piece of paper on the table which read, "Help me." Security came by the lab and informed Raj that the building was closed and there was no after-hours working authorized. Raj had no choice but to leave the building. As he was driving back home, there was heavy fog on the road. Suddenly, out of nowhere, he saw the same woman from the lab standing on the road; it was the same woman from the dreams. He stepped on the brakes but still hit the woman. He panicked and came to a stop. He ran out looking on the road, but there was no one there, only fog and total silence in the air.

Raj returned to his vehicle. His adrenalin on high, he drove off. While driving for about thirty seconds, he looked in the mirror, and he saw the woman sitting on the back seat, looking back at him through the mirror. Raj cried out and said, "What do you want from me?" He took his eyes off the road for a few seconds and lost control of the car just for a few seconds while looking into the mirror. He managed somehow to avoid an accident. He looked back into the back seat after making a controlled stop, and the woman again was gone. Raj finally got home without any further visions. And being drained from his evening's events, he slept without having dinner or speaking with his wife.

That night, Raj woke up from the sound of his wife's voice calling him, and he saw her sitting on a chair, silently staring at him without blinking an eye. Raj asked her, "Meena, what happened?" There was no answer from her, and Raj repeated the question, and once again, Meena did not answer him. A pause of about fifteen seconds or so, Meena said, in a solemn voice "I'm not Meena. I'm Muskaan." Raj was shivering with fear and asked. "Who's Muskaan?" Then Muskaan began to speak freely.

"I was the newest recruit in lab number 666. I was a forensic psychologist on the third floor. Dr. Kohli had his eyes on me from day one. He abused me often and became his test subject for some mad biowarfare weapon he was working on. My life was unbearable, and I had no one I could turn to for help. One day he, crossed all limits. He touched me in my office, abused me and then tied me to a chair and injected a chemical into my neck.

"I started to hallucinate and started seeing weird monsters, ghouls, etc. He was experimenting on a chemical that would cause fear in the people who were injected with that chemical. Many people have died under his homemade treatments. He tested on the asylum patients, and when they died, he disposed of the bodies. I do not know where.

"But when he saw he had no one else to experiment on, he used me instead. One day, I threatened him. I told him I will tell all of his secrets to the police and newspapers. He killed me and then set the floor on fire to destroy all evidence. I died in the fire. Ever since then, I was trapped in that room, waiting for my revenge. I want you to help me. Otherwise, I will kill your wife," said the voice of the woman. Raj, who loved his wife so dearly, agreed. Right after that last sentence, Raj decided to help. The woman left his wife's body, and she was looking at Raj and asking him how she got on the chair. Raj told her she just got up out of bed and sat there. Raj, being as brave as he can be, wondered how he would help this spirit out. What was in store for Raj now? If he told anyone of this, no one would believe him.

The next day, Raj went to Dr. Kohli and said, "She's back, and we need to close that door before she hurts anyone."

"Who's back?" asked Dr. Kohli.

"Muskaan."

"Impossible! There is no life after death, and you, as a scientist, know this."

"Well, you are wrong. I know all about you and the biochemical experiments you have been conducting, all the deaths from the experiments you performed, and the whereabouts of the bodies you got rid of."

Dr. Kohli, with fear in his eyes, went to the third floor with Raj, and when Dr. Kohli was going to lock the door with a new lock, the door swung open, and something pulled him in. And like in the movies, the door closed shut tight, and Raj was unable to open it. Suddenly, the door opened, and Raj saw the doctor on the chair, unable to move. *"Raj, help me. Raj!"* Suddenly, the doctor was turning white with fear; he was looking at Muskaan, and she was looking at him with those burning red eyes. Dr. Kohli said, "I thought you were dead. How did you manage to return?"

:I am dead, you fool, and it's all because of you," the woman answered.

"I am sorry, Muskaan, I shouldn't have done this to you. Please let me go," cried Dr. Kohli. You like to experiment, don't you? Let me give you a taste of your own medicine!" the woman shouted at Dr. Kohli. Then the doctor started to cry in pain and terror. Raj wasn't able to see anything that would cause him pain. Whatever Muskaan was doing to him was not visible, but the doctor was in hell. There was nothing that Raj could do, and the cell phone did not work inside because of all the surrounding metal in the room. The doctor was going to see the afterlife. The enigmas of the afterlife were unveiling. Dr. Kohli began to turn a light blue as if he could not breathe. All at once, he started to show multiple bruises on his face and was starting to have bloody eyes. His hands were lacerated, and suddenly within a few moments, Dr. Kohli was in flames. Raj was terrorized at what he just witnessed. He would never forget. He ran out trying to close the door, but he couldn't. It seemed like Muskaan was keeping it open and Dr. Kohli was not going anywhere. Raj was running out of the building and pulled the fire alarm on the way out and then stood outside watching the building being engulfed in flames with the doctor inside while the others managed to escape.

Muskaan finally got her revenge. Raj never told the story to anyone, even to his wife. He said to his wife there was a terrible accident at the lab, and the doctor was involved and died there. As things settled down on an normal level for the couple, Raj received a call from his neighbor to get home fast. "Your wife is dead." Raj rushed home, and there was a massive crowd of people outside his apartment. Raj was pushing through the group and heard that his wife had fallen from the apartment's top floor and was lying dead on the street.

"*Meena, No, no, no!* You can't leave me!" cried Raj and hugged his wife's covered body.

Raj was devastated and could find no reason why she would do this until he has gone back up to the apartment of theirs and found a note with a blue pen near the marriage photo of Raj and Meena, saying, "From Muskaan. This is for you trying to lock me back in the room with the doctor." When he picked up the pen, it had the letter *K* carved on it.

Is this story true or false?

Notes

Mr. Mohith S. Yadav

Biography

I taught forensics not by watching TV series but by reading real forensic science books, journals, and learning courses. My love for photography led to the learning of forensic photography. Learned fingerprints (the world of loops, arches, and whorls) trained in dusting, lifting and interpreting results in reports. I visited crime scenes, examined the evidence, and opinions were submitted to the police department. My pistol-shooting passion got my attention in ballistics, and I became a member of the Karnataka State Rifle Association.

I completed the majority of training in body fluid identification and DNA analysis.

I trained in the analysis of toxicology samples like alcohol, drugs, food forensics, and the results leading to a conclusion acceptable to experts in the field.

I trained in interpreting analytical results, postmortem reports, forensic science laboratory reports, and prepared written opinion reports. I could also testify as an expert witness in courts of law.

I was forensic genealogy trained with real genealogists, helps in missing persons, cold cases, and many more. Investigating cold cases is a booster to my brain. Hackers scared me, so I started learning ethical hacking, cyberforensics, tools used in recovery data, mobile device hacking, authentication of videos and photos that get viral in social media, analysis of CCTV footage. Victim assistance is my most vital unique selling point. I assisted in many trauma victims from domestic violence, physical abuse, sexual assault, and others.

Teaching to the next generation is one in many of my passions. My teachers taught me so many tricks. I am interested in passing on to the next gen. My research paper got published titled "Forensic Investigation of Cheap Liquors in Karnataka: Case Studies," which can be accessed at https://medicolegalreporter.com/page/current-issue.

The Disappearing Villagers

Mohith S Yadav

Rajasthan is one of the most haunted places in India. The Paliwal Brahmins inhabit it; Paliwal is known for its religious beliefs since its origins in the thirteenth century. Their ancestors emigrated to western Rajasthan and founded a vast community with their temples and adjacent villages. Later, other families moved to neighboring locations, where *Paliwals* (patriarchs) were still in control of that area. Nearly eighteen kilometers from Jaisalmer's, a delightful city near Rajasthan and Kuldhara villages, has been known for being abandoned by a thousand villagers in a single night. Rajasthan and Kuldhara were left due to a high level of paranormal activity. Rajasthan is one of the well-known haunted hot spots in the area. The villagers have said they could still hear the horrors of screaming and crying from the spirits after the Raksha Bandhan attacked the Mughal. One night, it was told that its occupants surrendered to Raksha Bandhan and were brutally slaughtered by Jaisalmer's village pastor Salim Singh. Hearing nothing but screams of terror and crying, sounds of running footsteps can also be heard nearly every night.

Rajasthan is in a desert region known for its ghost stories and treasure hidden somewhere in the village. Many people in the surrounding area who have known about this location believe that all these stories being told were to frighten the village people from finding any of the gold or other treasures buried somewhere in the village. Travelers have been warned to stay away from this town for their good and were told about the paranormal activities.

Travelers who visited the area have been telling the new travelers they have seen a woman wearing a white saree and showing up out of nowhere around the incineration ground. If they have plans on going to the ghost town of Bhangarh, they should be prepared because it is one of the most frightening, spookiest spots one could imagine and probably the most haunted place in India. They saw people who have died and were walking around as if they were still alive and carrying on business as usual.

Chawl (residential buildings) was built in a populated territory in Mahim. The people in Mumbai said they had seen an apparition of a young woman who stalks the area, crying and trying to communicate with people, and they do not respond to her. Maybe she does not know she is dead every evening at the same time; she then suddenly disappears once the sun comes up.

This phantom town is currently a traveler's site and subject to spooky occurrences. It was said that when you travel early in the morning through Delhi's separated and prosperous region, you will have the experience of seeing this same woman in a white saree walking around, looking for help.

Salim Singh, Mumbai's ruler, wanted to marry this woman from Mahim, and he threatened the village community's people and her father that he would take her away if they did not give her to him for a wife. So, village leader and the father of this girl from this village decided that Singh will not have her no matter what Singh demanded.

The father summoned all the surrounding residents of five villages to a meeting. During the meeting, one of the villagers said if Singh takes the girl, the villagers would come and fight to save her and her family from him no matter what it takes. The girl was like a queen in the town, and the family was well respected; and if it meant to go to war with Singh, it would happen.

Singh quietly entered the village one night and took the girl anyways despite the threats of the father and villagers given him, and he disappeared with her. Later, rumor has it that Singh had killed her and had spread her body parts all over in different village locations. Since then, terrifying events had been happening all around the village, such as sounds of a screaming woman, saying, "Singh stop, stop!" and more screams. Sounds of chopping wood and then seeing a nearly transparent woman in a white saree walking around in the village happen as well. Many believe it was the young woman Singh took haunting the town.

When I arrived in the village, I saw a man with sunken eyes with a long black beard who asked me to sit with him. With nervousness, I said, okay. The man started to tell me about the ghost town's tragic story. The man said it seemed that this village was still waiting for its family, friends, and villagers to return and let the town flourish again. He started to tell me about the town having a curse placed on it, then he just suddenly stopped talking. The older man then got up, and as I turned my head for a split second and looked back at him, he vanished. I guess all the stories that have been told were right because I think I just talked to one of them. Travelers coming into the peaceful and un-haunted village have been warned not to travel into the haunted villages at night. Even paranormal hunters from Delhi say that as dusk falls outside the small temple in the village of Kuldhara, there are sounds of stomping feet and anklets jingling, loud and whispering voices, humanlike shadows walking around, and the sound of running and then walking footsteps on the ground. There have been reports in Kuldhara, and not even a soul was present in the church because of the fear of walking at night and being a victim of the dead.

Still, thirty people are living there, defying the so-called curse that the village is said to have. Rumor has it that the town, in 1825, placed the curse on it by the villagers themselves. It has also been reported that after leaving this village, no one could ever return, nor can anyone ever move there. And if they did move there, they would die very soon. The residents that had cast the curse on this town said anyone who tries to move into the village would die quickly after or vanish without a sign.

The villages are still abandoned to the present date. It is most likely because the villages are still being haunted, and no one has ever dared to come here and visit. People who did ignore the curse and walked during the night had disappeared and were never seen again.

One of the villagers asked what brought me there. I said my curiosity took me here. The man said, "You must want to die then." I told the man, "No, because I am not moving here but only curious about the stories told." I came from Delhi to investigate this haunting place at night. I was talking to a man who lived here and worked as a cafeteria caretaker. He said to me that he and his family had lived here for many years, and there was nothing unusual about this place. Another male worker for the same cafeteria who lived there stated that he had lived there for over twenty years and never heard about this curse. After talking to him for a few minutes, I walk back to my vehicle, thinking if this guy could live here, why does legend say no one can live here? The story has it that the villagers who did leave took what they could carry on their backs and leaving only their memories and the unstoppable curse behind.

Later, a gruesome discovery of murdered bodies found in the woods surrounding the nearby schools erupted. A few local people and some vacationers reported being chased by a headless person believing to be a young boy from one of the schools, and then he vanishes into the forest. While driving by the woods along the roadside, people also reported seeing bodies lying by the road, and when they exited the vehicle to walk back to the spot where they saw the bodies, they were gone. Since then, no one has lived in the village, and the cursed town kept quiet. It is being said that people who have visited the village at night experienced strange paranormal sightings and hearing such sounds as screams, crying, and saw transparent beings trying to hide from the living. Some said they have seen transparent figures walking and running as if someone was chasing them along the roadside. Some were even looking for a ride. One other person said there was a woman in her sixties that was crying for help along the side of the road, and as they were getting closer to her, they could see right through her; and them seeing this, they just kept on driving and terrified. Not one person in this nearby ghost town had seen over a thousand individuals leaving the village that one single night, and until now, nobody knows what happened to them or where Paliwals had gone. It was as if they just vanished in thin air. Many people outside of Kuldhara said that Kuldhara is a village of ghosts, and anyone living there will soon die because of the curse put on the town. Kuldhara Rajasthan, a former castle built in the early nineteenth century and bearing buildings from the 1980s, is one of India's most haunted places. Today, it is home to India's most popular tourist attractions. Gaurav Tiwari of the Indian

Paranormal Society, who died in 2016, claims to have recorded these strange events—in Kuldhara. Are they true? Only Gaurav Tiwari of the Indian Paranormal Society knows.

Notes

You Can Purchase Online Paranormal Ghost-Hunting Equipment

Advanced GQ EMF-390 Multi-Field, Multi-Function
EMF Meter and RF Spectrum Power Analyzer With
Data Logger (Patent Pending)
Internet Prices range from $137.00 to $150.00
https://www.youtube.com/
watch?v=P7WDQrIBDHw&pbjreload=101

Night Vision Binoculars (Internet prices range from $10 to $16.)

Meterk EMF Meter Handheld Mini Digital LCD EMF Detector
Electromagnetic Field Radiation Tester Dosimeter Tester Counter
(Internet prices range from $18 to $21)

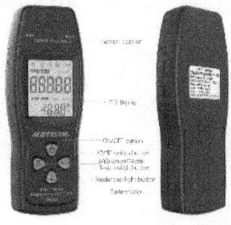

https://www.youtube.com/watch?v=FWA3eTRnksc&pbjreload=101
(Courtesy photo by Meterk)

Assist with shielding yourself from the harmful EMF signals and frequencies. The EMF Shield is a corrective, harmonizing resonance triple-patented proprietary technology designed to assist the body with counterbalancing these negative frequencies from computers, phones, microwaves, monitors, and Wi-Fi devices. Simply place the EMF Shield close to the power source to protect you, and your family. (Internet prices range from $35 to $42)

(Courtesy Photo by The EMF Shield)

Spirit Box SB11 Ghost-Hunting Equipment Radio Sweep Ghost Box
    The PSB11 has again and again been used on paranormal TV shows and on investigations and have created remarkable EVPs that relates to the investigated site. It sweeps radio frequencies much faster than other ghost boxes. The white noise and the fast scanning of radio frequencies is believed to provide the energy and transmission that spirits need to get their voices through to us. Internet prices range from $130 to $142.
https://www.youtube.com/watch?v=34yf_MbW0nk&pbjreload=101

Courtesy photo by NUATE

320 × 240 IR Resolution Thermal Camera, Pocket-Sized Infrared Camera with 76800 Pixels Real-Time Thermal Image, Temperature Measurement Range -4°F to 572°F, Mini IR Thermal Imager, Hti-Xintai. (Internet prices range from $130 to $142.)

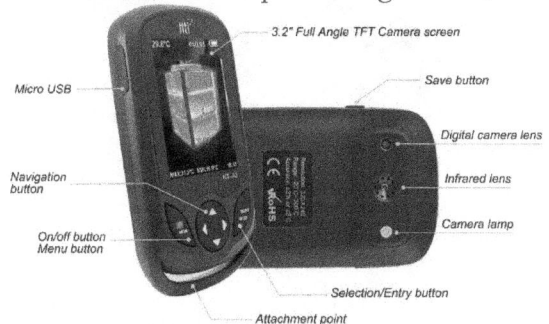

HT-A2 THERMAL IMAGING IMAGE DISPLAY

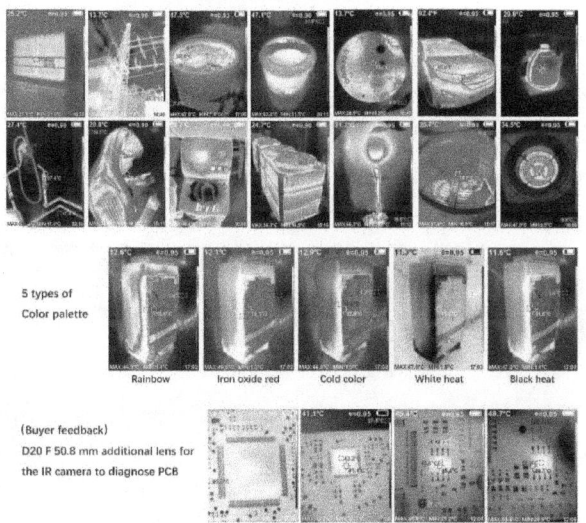

Courtesy Photo by Hti-Xintai
https://www.youtube.com/watch?v=9Q9PFX2ey6s&pbjreload=101
Ultimate Ghost-Hunting Kit + EMF Meter + EVP
Recorder + Laser Grid Pen X2 + More
Internet prices range from $180 to $195.

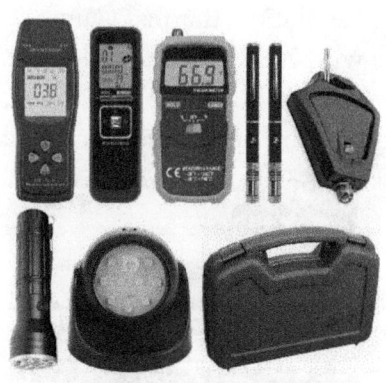

Courtesy Photo by www.ebay.com
https://www.ebay.com/i/163726943034
Ultimate Ghost-Hunting Kit

Digital LCD EMF Meter. This digital EMF meter has a large and clear LCD display with an option to choose either *milligauss* or *microtesla* scale. It features a *settable sound/light alarm* that can be adjusted as low as 1.0 milligauss to alert you of any unusual EMF readings. The alarm will make a beeping sound and the display will turn red. This is very useful if you want to set the meter down in a room and continue investigating other rooms of a building. The sound alarm will alert you of any *EMF spikes* without having to view the display. There is also an option to mute the sound alarm if so desired. Another great feature is a manual *backlight option* to make viewing of the LCD display easier in very dark conditions. Other functions include an auto power off option to save battery life when not in use and a *battery strength indicator* to let you know when the batteries need to be replaced. Spirits are theorized to emit electromagnetic fields and if you watch any of the *ghost-hunting TV shows*, you will know that *EMF spikes* are a very good indication of spirit activity. This is why a good quality EMF meter is so important to have while doing paranormal research! Every paranormal investigator should own at least one meter that measures electromagnetic fields!

Measuring EMF spikes is crucial for documenting evidence of spirit activity!

https://www.youtube.com/watch?v=CNm9eVYC9z0

Digital EVP Recorder

This is a PCM Digital EVP Recorder with *8gb* of flash memory that *records in **ultra high quality** .wav format at 384k bps* (see all recorder specs below). PCM (pulse code modulation) technology is a means by which standard audio signals are converted to digital audio signals. It is powered by two AAA alkaline batteries (included) which is much more conducive for paranormal research than recorders powered by a rechargeable battery pack! Spirits can drain batteries and standard batteries are easy to replace while out in the field or investigating anywhere! *WAV recording format is much higher quality than MP3 format* used on many recorders! Most MP3 recorders only have a maximum recording quality of 192k bps! We highly recommend using a digital EVP recorder that is powered by standard batteries and records in ultrahigh quality format! Transfer your saved audio files to your computer with the *included USB cable*! An external microphone is included but we find that the *built-in dual microphones* work just as well and are much easier to use for capturing EVPs while ghost hunting! A good quality digital EVP recorder that records in ultra high-quality format is a must have for any serious paranormal investigator!

High-quality recording is essential for capturing electronic voice phenomena!

https://www.youtube.com/watch?v=pgb3B1TgQ6s&pbjreload=101
Similar to this one

Green Laser Grid Pen

This two-in-one green laser pen has a single laser beam (remove end cap) and a laser grid that *can be adjusted for various patterns* by twisting the end cap. The single laser beam is great for pointing things out to fellow investigators and the laser grid can be used to detect any movement from spirits. Any disruption in the grid pattern can be seen with the naked eye or can be captured on video! *Shadow people* are believed to be spirits with dense energy and can easily be detected with a laser grid! A momentary push button switch is used to activate the laser but we include a *rubber o-ring* that can be fitted over the pen to hold down the button for a *hands-free laser grid*. We recommend rechargeable AAA batteries if you are going to be using the laser pen for prolonged use! This portable laser pen is high powered *(5mw)*, extremely bright and very durable! This is a piece of equipment that no paranormal investigator should be without!

Laser grid pens are used by experienced paranormal investigators to detect shadow people!
https://www.youtube.com/watch?v=eBX0ut0z62U&pbjreload=101

Digital LCD Thermometer

This is a thermocouple microprocessor thermometer that *measures ambient air temperature* at a very fast rate of two samples per second! It features a modified k-type thermocouple sensor that plugs in on the top of the thermometer like you would find on a Mel Meter and is very sensitive to fluctuations of ambient air temperature! It has a large LCD display and shows temperature readings with decimal point (example: 63.7 degrees). There is a function to switch from Celsius or Fahrenheit and also a hold button if you want to lock in a temperature reading. We would like to explain the difference between an infrared noncontact thermometer (sometimes called a laser thermometer) and a thermocouple thermometer. A thermocouple thermometer has a metal wire sensor that measures ambient air temperature (room air temperature) at the point where the sensor is located at time of temperature reading. This is the way our thermometer works as well as some other popular thermometers/multi-meters for paranormal research like the Mel Meter.

An infrared noncontact thermometer (some gun shaped, mini *cen-tech* and others) emits a laser beam as a guide and measures the infrared energy of the first *solid/liquid* object that the beam hits. The infrared energy of that object is then converted to a surface temperature reading by the thermometer. So let's say you are investigating in a room somewhere and you suddenly feel a cold spot, you would want to take a temperature reading of the room air temperature near where you are located, right? If you use a thermocouple thermometer, then you will get a *true ambient air temperature reading*! If you use an infrared noncontact thermometer and aim it towards a wall, then you will only get a surface temperature reading of the wall itself! There are "theories" on how an infrared thermometer may be useful for ghost hunting but none that make any sense to us. We have even seen some sellers say that their infrared non-contact thermometer measures ambient air temperature which is simply *not true at all*! We are just giving you *the facts* and in our opinion a thermocouple thermometer is much more conducive for paranormal research! *Measuring a sudden drop in air temperature is a very effective way to document spirit activity!*

https://www.youtube.com/
results?search_query=Digital+LCD+Thermometer&pbjreload=102

Any one of these will work:

Multipurpose Flashlight

This three-in-one multipurpose flashlight has 10 white light LEDs, *five ultraviolet light LEDs* and a single red laser beam. The white light LEDs are great as a normal flashlight for finding your way around in the dark. The ultraviolet LEDs are excellent for *blacklight* illumination when necessary or just a non-bright light. We have found that using an *ultraviolet light source* with a night vision camera or camcorder illuminates much better than in regular infrared night shot mode. The laser beam pointer comes in very handy for pointing things out to fellow investigators. The flashlight case is made from *solid aircraft aluminum* and is very durable! We never do an investigation without these flashlights!

Some paranormal investigators have a theory that ultraviolet light may actually attract spirits!

https://www.youtube.com/watch?v=olgcKX0XowU

Infrared Motion Sensor

This motion sensor is very sensitive to movement and is perfect for paranormal investigations! In auto mode, it illuminates automatically when motion is detected within a *12ft/120 degree radius* in front of the sensor and turns off automatically twenty-five to thirty seconds after motion ceases. A built-in photocell prevents activation during daylight hours and in brightly lit locations. It also has a built-in passive infrared sensor that *detects heat signatures* within the detection range. The round motion sensor light can rotate in any direction and can be removed from the base. It can also be *used as a flashlight* by setting to the On position. This motion sensor does not have an audio alarm but we believe this is actually much better for paranormal investigations. Motion sensors with alarms are usually *extremely loud* and can corrupt any EVP recordings! We usually set up a night vision DVR to record any activity from the motion sensor or place it in a spot where we can watch it without setting it off ourselves. We find these motion sensors to be very useful for collecting evidence of any spirit activity!

Motion sensors are used by most paranormal investigators to detect unseen movement by spirits!

https://www.youtube.com/watch?v=a4e2wG0igsc&pbjreload=101

You do not have to settle with this sensor

Red LED Keychain Light

This red LED keychain light is great for preserving your night vision during paranormal investigations!

Your eyes can take up to thirty minutes to adjust to the dark and any *white light will ruin your night vision* almost instantly. Red light has no effect on night vision and this compact red LED light comes in very handy for investigating in very dark conditions!

Information here was provided by eBay sold by paranormal-ITC

Glossary of Paranormal Terms

Abductee. Person who claims to have been abducted by an extraterrestrial.

Achluophobia. Fear of darkness.

Aeromancy. The art of predicting the future by observing atmospheric events such as wind and cloud formations (a.k.a. austromancy).

Agateophobia. Fear of insanity.

Alchemy. An ancient pseudoscience involving the study of transmuting metals, in particular, turning base metals into gold. Alchemy is also symbolic of human transformation into higher states of existence.

Alien. An extraterrestrial being, i.e., from some location other than the earth.

Angel.

1. Spiritual being superior to man in power and intelligence.

2. An attendant spirit or guardian.

3. A white-robed winged figure of human form.

Animal PSI. The apparent ability of animals to exhibit psychic powers such as clairvoyance, telepathy and even psychokinesis.

Apparition. A supernatural manifestation of a person (dead or living), animals or objects. Ghosts are apparitions of dead people.

Apport. An object or living being that materializes from thin air in the presence of a medium.

Archangel. Elder or higher-ranking angels who are said to guide the spiritual lives of populations of people, rather than individuals who are tended to by angels.

Astral.

1. Of relating to, or coming from the stars,

2. Of or consisting of a supersensible substance held in theosophy to be next above the tangible world in refinement.

Athazagoraphobia. Fear of being forgotten or ignored or forgetting.

Automatonophobia. Fear of ventriloquist's dummies, animatronics creatures, and wax statues—anything that falsely represents a sentient being.

Bewitch.

1. To influence or affect especially injuriously by witchcraft; to cast a spell over.

2. To attract as if by the power of witchcraft: *enchant.*

Bogyphobia. Fear of bogeys or the bogeyman.

Clairaudience. The power or faculty of hearing something not present to the ear but regarded as having objective reality.

Clairvoyance.

1. The power or faculty of discerning objects not present to the senses.

2. Ability to perceive matters beyond the range or ordinary perception.

Conjure. To summon a devil or spirit by invocation or incantation; to practice magical arts.

Conjurer.

1. One that practices magic arts: *wizard,*

2. One that performs feats of sleight of hand and illusion.

Cross-quarter days. Sabbaths falling between the solstices and equinoxes: Samhain, Imbolc, Beltane, and Lughnasadh.

Coven. An organized group of Wiccans sometimes restricted to thirteen members.

Déjà vu. An unexpected sense of familiarity to what is believed to be a new experience, place, person, or object.

Demon (Daemon).

1. An evil spirit; a source or agent of evil, harm, distress or ruin.

2. An attendant power or spirit 3: a supernatural being of Greek mythology intermediate between gods and men.

Demoniac.

1. Possessed of influenced by a demon.

2. Of relating to, or suggestive of a demon: fiendish.

Demonic, Demonology.

1. The study of demons or evil spirits

2. Belief in demons.

Elements. Wiccan: air, water, earth, fire, and spirit. A Wiccan's world is viewed of in terms of four physical elements—earth, water, air, and fire (which roughly correspond to the four scientific forms of matter: solid, liquid, gas, and plasma)—plus spirit. Together, these elements form a united whole, as is symbolized in the pentagram. All are necessary and should be in balance.

Elementals. A supernatural entity or force thought to be physically manifested by occult means.

Elf.

1. A small often mischievous fairy.

2. A small lively creature; also, a usually lively mischievous or malicious person.

Enchant.

1. To influence by or as if by charms and incantation: *bewitch.*

2. To attract and move deeply rouse to ecstatic admiration.

Enchantment.

1. The act or art of enchanting; the quality or state of being enchanted.

2. Something that enchants.

Equinox. Around March 22 and September 22, when day and night are equal in length. Held as the Sabbaths of Ostara and Mabon.

Esbat. A celebration that takes place during the full moon each month.

ESP (extrasensory perception). Perception (as in telepathy, clairvoyance, and precognition) that involves awareness of information about events external to the self not gained through the senses and not deducible from previous experience.

Fairy. A mythical being of folklore and romance usually having diminutive human form and magic powers.

Ghost (noun).

1. The seat of life or intelligence; soul.

2. A disembodied soul; the soul of a dead person believed to be an inhabitant of the unseen world or to appear to the living in bodily likeness.

3. A spirit or demon.

4. A faint shadowy trace; the least bit.

5. False image in a photographic negative or on a television screen caused by reflection.

6. One who ghostwrites

7. A red blood cell that has lost its hemoglobin.

Ghost (verb).

1. To haunt like a ghost.

2. To move silently; to sail quietly in light winds.

Hag.

1. An ugly, slatternly, or evil-looking old woman.

2. Archaic; a female demon; an evil or frightening spirit; hobgoblin.

3. Witch.

Haunt.

1. To visit or inhabit as a ghost.

2. To stay around; to appear habitually as a ghost.

3. A place habitually frequented by ghosts.

Hemophobia, hemaphobia, hematophobia. Fear of blood.

Hereditary witch. Someone who has passed the skills of witchcraft down through his or her family.

Hobgoblin. A mischievous goblin.

Incubus. A demon or goblin which appears as a male mortal seeking to seduce women, usually while they sleep. A feeling that a familiar place or situation has never been experienced before.

Jamais vu. A feeling that a familiar place or situation has never been experienced before.

Kirlian photography. Named after Seymon Kirlian, a controversial technique to photograph a person's aura or biofield.

Levitation. The raising of a body into the air without physical aid.

Ley lines. Patterns and alignments of invisible energy said to connect various sacred locations, e.g., churches, stone circles, burial grounds, etc.

Lucifer. The name of Satan before his fall from heaven.

Lycanthropy. In folklore, the ability of a person to change into animal form. In psychiatry, the delusion of having been transformed into an animal.

Magic.

1. The use of means (as charms or spells) believed to have supernatural power over natural forces; magic rites or incantations.

2. An extraordinary power or influence seemingly from a supernatural source; something that seems to cast a spell: *enchantment.*

3. The art of producing illusions by sleight of hand.

Medium. An individual held to be a channel of communication between the earthly world and the world of spirits.

Necromancy.

1. Conjuration of the spirits of the dead for purposes of magically revealing the future or influencing the course of events.

2. *Magic, sorcery.*

Necrophilia. Fear of death or dead things.

Neo-pagan. Another name for pagan.

Nyctophobia. Fear of the dark or of night.

Orb. A type of anomaly that appears in photographs, especially digital flash photography, in which mysterious objects appear floating in the air.

Out-of-body. Relating to or involving a feeling of separation from one's body and of being able to view oneself and others from an external perspective.

Pagan. (Middle English, from Late Latin *paganus*, from Latin, country dweller, from *pagus* country district; akin to Latin *pang* ere to fix; follower of an Earth Religion. All Wiccans are *pagans*.

Paganism. Any polytheistic religion or any non-Judeo-Christian religion. However, both of these definitions include such people as Hindus and Amerindians, neither of which associate their religious practices with paganism.

Paranormal. Not scientifically explainable. Supernatural.

Parapsychology. Is the study of alleged psychic phenomena (extrasensory perception, as in telepathy, precognition, clairvoyance, psychokinesis, a.k.a. telekinesis, and psychometry) and other paranormal claims; for example related to near-death experiences, synchronicity, apparitional experiences, etc.

Paraskavedekatriaphobia. Fear of Friday the 13th.

Pediophobia. Fear of dolls.

Pentagram. A symbol of protection and invocation. Always depicted point up. Symbolizes the union of the five basic elements.

Phenomenon.

1. An observable fact or event.

2. An object or aspect known through the senses rather than by thought or intuition; a temporal or spatiotemporal object of sensory experience as distinguished from a noumenon; a fact or event of scientific interest susceptible of scientific description and explanation

3. A rare or significant factor event b plural phenomenon; an exceptional, unusual, or abnormal person, thing, or occurrence.

Poltergeist. A noisy usually mischievous ghost held to be responsible for unexplained noises.

Precognition. To know beforehand: clairvoyance relating to an event or state not yet experienced.

Psychic.

1. Of or relating to the psyche.

2. Lying outside the sphere of physical science or knowledge; immaterial, moral, or spiritual in origin or force

3. Sensitive to nonphysical or supernatural forces and influences; marked by extraordinary or mysterious sensitivity, perception, or understanding.

Psychokinesis. Movement of physical objects by the mind without use of physical means.

Psychometric. Divination of facts concerning an object or its owner through contact with or proximity to the object.

Sorcerer. A person who practices sorcery; wizard.

Sorcery.

1. The use of power gained from the assistance or control of evil spirits especially for divining; *necromancy.*

2. Magic.

Soul. The immaterial essence, animating principle, or actuating cause of an individual life; the spiritual principle embodied in human beings, all rational and spiritual beings, or the universe.

Spirit.

1. An animating or vital principle held to give life to physical organisms.

2. A supernatural being or essence, as a: Holy Spirit; Soul; an often malevolent being that is bodiless but can become visible; a malevolent being that enters and possesses a human being.

Spirit (verb). To carry off usually secretly or mysteriously.

Spiritualism.

1. The view that spirit is a prime element of reality.

2. A belief that spirits of the dead communicate with the living usually through a medium; a movement comprising of religious organization emphasizing spiritualism.

Sprite.

1. An archaic: *soul*; A disembodied spirit: *ghost*.

2. *Elf, fairy*; an elfish person.

Succubus. A female demon or goblin which appears as a female mortal seeking to seduce men, usually while they sleep.

Supernatural.

1. Of or relating to an order of existence beyond the visible observable universe; of or relating to God or a god, demigod, spirit or devil.

2. Departing from what is usual or normal especially so as to appear to transcend the laws of nature; attributed to an invisible agent (as a ghost or spirit).

Taphophilia. A passion for and enjoyment of cemeteries.

Telekinesis. The production of motion in objects without contact or other physical means.

Telepathy. Communication from one mind to another by extrasensory means.

Vampire.

1. The reanimated body of a dead person believed to come from the grave at night and suck the blood of persons asleep.

2. One who lives by preying on others; a woman who exploits and ruins her lover.

Zombie. The supernatural power that according to voodoo belief may enter into and reanimate a dead body; a will-less, speechless human capable only of automatic movement who is held to have died and supernaturally reanimated.

CPSIA information can be obtained
at www.ICGtesting.com
Printed in the USA
BVHW030833030621
608729BV00010B/2217/J